Tom Cox's writing has appeared in the *Daily Telegraph*, *Sunday Times*, *Observer*, *Mail on Sunday*, *Jack* magazine, *The Times* and the *Guardian*, for which paper he was Pop Critic between 1999 and 2000. He is the author of two books: *Nice Jumper* which was shortlisted for the 2002 National Sporting ⋯⋯ Best Newcomer Award, and *Educating Peter*. He was ⋯⋯⋯⋯⋯ and lives with his wife in Norfolk.

Acclaim for *Ed*

'A music memoi

'A funny insight ⋯⋯⋯⋯⋯ *irror*

'Brilliant ... the ⋯⋯⋯⋯⋯ hat land of lost discontent (teena⋯⋯, ⋯⋯⋯⋯⋯ Julie Burchill, *Guardian*

'A charming account of how boys and young men learn to define themselves' *GQ*

'A brilliantly funny odyssey and insight into the teenage male psyche' *Publishing News*

'His rock knowledge is impeccable; the overall effect is oddly endearing' *Observer*

Acclaim for *Nice Jumper:*

'The Fever Putt of golf, an engaging tale of sporting obsession and adolescent fumbling for identity ... consistently entertaining and often extremely funny ... "Is golf sort of like, really boring, Tom?" asks a girlfriend. "Well, yeah and no," he replies. In Cox's hands, very much the latter' Martin Fletcher, *Independent*

'*Nice Jumper* captures both the intoxicating sense of being "the one" and the icy douche of adulthood that soon follows. Thank the Lord for those crazy dreams, and the writers, such as Cox, who can make us laugh at them ... an enormously fun read' *The Times*

'*Nice Jumper* does for golf what *Fever Pitch* did for football ... it's funny, clever and all-too-horribly true' William Boyd

'At last a book about growing up populated by characters who aren't entirely hateful. In fact *Nice Jumper* is knitted with real warmth and passion, my two favourite things apart from wanking and Bowie. And the golf stuff isn't a problem'
Adam Buxton, of Adam and Joe

'Extremely funny – often laugh-out-loud funny, occasionally a threat to the intercostal muscles ... a large fizzy can of Diet Hornby'   Mel Webb, *The Times*

'He'll probably do more here to interest the non-putting fraternity in the sport than Tiger Woods and P G Wodehouse put together'
Guardian

'Hilarious true story about an East Midlands teenager, ignoring the traditional lure of cider, ecstasy and music for the world of golf and the Cripsley Edge golf club. Lashings of insight, sarcasm and slapstick. Fore!'   *Jack*

'*Nice Jumper* is certain to strike a chord with most golfers – it's funny and it's well written'   *Sunday Times*

'Hugely enjoyable début ... *Nice Jumper* treads similar ground to *The Commitments* and *Fever Pitch*, but with a depth and humour very much of its own. Recommended'   *The Leeds Guide*

'A charming and funny coming of age story ... this book, as Julie Burchill pithily observes on the cover, can be described as "*The Catcher in the Rye* meets *Caddyshack*"'
The Times Literary Supplement

'An enjoyable look at childhood obsessions told with an amusing self-deprecation that makes you turn the pages all the quicker'
Sunday Express

'This is a wry fable of sporting par-adise lost'   *Time Out*

Also by Tom Cox

NICE JUMPER

and published by Black Swan

EDUCATING PETER
TOM COX

BLACK SWAN

EDUCATING PETER
A BLACK SWAN BOOK: 0 552 77119 8

Originally published in Great Britain by Bantam Press,
a division of Transworld Publishers

PRINTING HISTORY
Bantam Press edition published 2003
Black Swan edition published 2004

1 3 5 7 9 10 8 6 4 2

Set in 11/13pt Melior by
Falcon Oast Graphic Art Ltd.

Black Swan Books are published by Transworld Publishers,
61–63 Uxbridge Road, London W5 5SA,
a division of The Random House Group Ltd,
in Australia by Random House Australia (Pty) Ltd,
20 Alfred Street, Milsons Point, Sydney, NSW 2061, Australia,
in New Zealand by Random House New Zealand Ltd,
18 Poland Road, Glenfield, Auckland 10, New Zealand
and in South Africa by Random House (Pty) Ltd,
Endulini, 5a Jubilee Road, Parktown 2193, South Africa.

Printed and bound in Great Britain by
Cox & Wyman Ltd, Reading, Berkshire.

Papers used by Transworld Publishers are natural, recyclable
products made from wood grown in sustainable forests. The
manufacturing processes conform to the environmental
regulations of the country of origin.

To Brewer

MAMA TOLD ME NOT TO STRUM

The way I remember it is something like this.

He drags himself into the room, eyes to the floor, hands buried in the arms of his long-sleeve t-shirt. Jenny says, 'Pete, meet Tom'; he mumbles hello. He roots around in the cupboard for a packet of crisps. I ask him what CDs he's bought recently; he mumbles something about the second AC/DC album. He shuffles away, back to his bedroom.

I say, 'So. I'll pick him up a week on Tuesday, then?'

Jenny says, 'If you could, that would be wonderful. He's got fencing class from ten till eleven, then he's all yours.'

I say, 'Right, er, cool. I guess I'll be off.'

Jenny says, 'Mind out for those roadworks on the North Circular.'

And that's how it all started.

Did I miss a bit out? Possibly. There's a chance he picked up one of his bass guitars and plucked disconsolately at it for thirty seconds before he rooted around for the crisps. Perhaps we even shook hands. What's pretty certain, however, is that our first meeting couldn't have been described as 'unforgettable'. Nothing screeched, sparked or went 'Kapow!' Nobody called the police or drove a 1969 Aston Martin.

Like many men who'd grown up playing with too many model cars and watching too many films starring Warren Oates, I'd often fantasised about this moment: the beginning of my Great Road Trip. I'd pictured Jeff Bridges haring out of nowhere in a Dodge Charger to save Clint Eastwood from a shower of bullets during the opening scene of *Thunderbolt And Lightfoot*. I'd pictured a big sky, a fast car, a hopelessly romantic meeting of inseparable outlaws, perhaps with the added bonus of a couple of loose women looking for a ride to nowhere in particular. But now this was it: I was here, finally embarking on my adventure, and all I could see was a North London kitchen, the first flowering of acne, some rather fetching Ikea units and a Slipknot t-shirt.

Outside the window, a wicked wind took a running jump down Alexander Palace hill, whipping along Crouch End Broadway, making a couple of local underfed aesthetes unsteady on their feet. Double-parked, my slightly-lower-than-middle-of-the-range Ford Fiesta waited for some action beyond the hot wax it had been lavished with earlier that day. Upstairs, in his room, the Thunderbolt to my Lightfoot attempted to master the riff to Metallica's 'Enter Sandman'. North London slept. Nothing continued to not happen. I decided, on balance, I'd settle for it.

Then again, by this point I would have settled for just about anything.

My whole life, I'd been planning some kind of four-wheeled journey into the unknown, but as the years piled up – that is, the years when it is still dignified to drive around for the hell of it while dressed in a loud shirt, listening to even louder music – my Great Rock And Roll Road Trip had become in danger of turning into My Great Bag Of Hot Air. The original idea had been something fairly vague that I'd dreamt up on receiving my first plastic pedal car as a seven-year-old: I would drive, anywhere, mindlessly, just for the thrill of driving. In my late teens, this was modified to the cliché of all Great Road Trip clichés: I would fly to New York, buy an ineffably cool second-hand car and drive cross-country to San Francisco, picking up hobos, buskers and itinerant jazz musicians on the way. However, in 1997, as I was travelling back from an Italian holiday, the plane had been struck by lightning, plummeting 1,000 terrifying feet before righting itself. As a result, I'd vowed not to take to the air for the foreseeable future, thus making America a less viable option. Additionally, I'd finally got around to reading Jack Kerouac's *On The Road*, rather than just talking about it, and discovered it was a vacuous pile of antelope droppings.

More recently, my thoughts had turned towards the winding B-roads and endless Little Chefs of my home-land. Everyone talked about the American Dream, but what about the British equivalent? Did it exist and, if so, what did it look like? How come you never saw rootless outlaw types cruising through the Lake District just for the existential hell of it? Was drifting banned in Britain, and had someone forgotten to tell me?

I wanted to discover the real Britain. Whatever this was, I felt certain it was out there: a rock and roll place every bit as weird as the backwoods America that writers like Hunter S. Thompson and Tom Wolfe had discovered. But more than anything I wanted an excuse to drive around aimlessly, getting lost in places with names like Snafbury and Little Piddling. All I needed was someone willing to ride shotgun: a relentlessly up-for-it soulmate – the kind of partner who'd be willing to help me out of a gambling debt, come to my aid in a tussle with Hell's Angels, or, more importantly, navigate me out of a council estate on the outskirts of Hull. But circumstances had changed since I'd begun to lay down the plans for my Great Rock And Roll Road Trip. Many of the friends who'd shared with me in the nihilist's vision of films like *Vanishing Point* and *Two-Lane Blacktop* as twenty-year-olds now held down steady jobs in insurance and the civil service. Most of them simply couldn't afford to up sticks and abandon their jobs and girlfriends for six months. The ones who could, meanwhile, just couldn't see the same romance in driving up the M4 listening to Fairport Convention as they'd once seen in cruising along Route 66 listening to The Byrds. There were still the isolated loose cannons I knew I could count on, of course: Colin and Surreal Ed, a couple of relentlessly cheerful womanisers with a penchant for jumping out of cars at red traffic lights and running into nearby woodland for no apparent reason. These, though, were the kind of insatiable single and free party animals for whom 'a good book and an early night' meant the latest issue of *Mayfair* and only two nightclubs instead of the normal four. In other words, great company in moderation but a veritable health hazard if you were talking about six months on the road, and not one I could afford as a married man with a mortgage and five pet cats to support.

In short, I was beginning to lose hope.

The call from Jenny couldn't have come at a more desperate moment. Jenny, I could be fairly certain, wasn't the type of woman who would jump out of your car at a red light and hide in adjacent shrubbery. She was fifty-three, for a start – the same age as my parents – and in full-time employment as a college lecturer. I'd known her since my third birthday party, when, seated in her lap, I'd smeared an ice cream sundae in her hair for reasons I can only remember as 'to see what it felt like'. Since then, I'd enjoyed the kind of respectfully distant relationship with her that one enjoys with surprisingly cool friends of one's family whom one has disgraced oneself in front of. I tended to see her, when it came right down to it, at fiftieth birthday parties and weddings. Jenny liked a lot of good blues music and, unlike many of my parents' other friends, still occasionally found time to go out to the cinema, but it had never occurred to me to call her up to arrange a friendly drink. You just didn't do that kind of thing with your parents' mates. Besides, she and her ex-husband, Ian, had their hands full with Peter, a teenage son whom I'd never met but who relatives assured me was just making the transition into the 'melancholy' stage of adolescence. For a couple of weeks now, my parents had been hinting that she might get in touch with me with a mysterious proposal, but I couldn't guess what it could possibly be.

'It's about that road trip you've been planning,' Jenny explained to me, after we'd caught up on some random family gossip.

'Oh. You heard about that? Bit of a non-starter, really.'

'Yes, well, I had a bit of an idea that I'd like to put to you that might make it a starter again.'

Abruptly, my mind filled with incongruous images of me and a flame-haired ex-hippie cruising along a sun-splashed highway, radio on, sunroof open, discussing the meaning of life. Part of me kind of liked the idea. Part of me didn't. The remainder was alive with questions. What would my wife think? Where could this journey possibly go? How many times would we have to stop at Ikea?

'It's to do with Pete,' continued Jenny.

I let out a silent lungful of relief. 'Oh yes? How old is he now?' I asked.

'Well, let me tell you all about him,' said Jenny.

And, for the next half an hour, she did.

Peter, Jenny explained, had recently turned fourteen and, virtually overnight, an unfathomable transformation had come over him. Just yesterday, it seemed, he'd been a cheery, fluffy-haired kid whose main priority in life had been where his next Pokemon toy was coming from; now he stalked the house in black clothes, guitar slung over his shoulder, a storm-cloud in trousers looking for somewhere to rain. The funny thing was, Jenny couldn't remember ever buying him any black clothes. And what were those strange dangly chains that hung from his trousers? Try as she might, she couldn't work out what had detonated the change in her son. It could have been a friend. It could have been a video or record he had heard. It could merely have been a new set of hormones. Peter certainly wasn't giving anything away. But he was certain about one thing: one day, in the not-too-distant future, he was going to be a rock star, and he wasn't going to let anything stand in his way.

Jenny didn't have anything against producing a rock musician, per se. She'd liked plenty of rock music when she was younger, and had even been on dates with a few of the hairy people who made it. But now, three or four months into her son's obsession, it was becoming obvious that it was having an adverse effect on his schoolwork. Peter's teachers were starting to use words like 'enigma' and 'unfulfilled'. And it got worse, said Jenny. Two weeks ago, Gaynor, the nanny Jenny relied on to look after Peter when she was off in Europe on lecture tours, had handed in her notice, having decided to go and work on a kibbutz in Israel. Meanwhile, Ian, who worked as an actor, was due to spend most of the summer as part of a travelling theatre on the American West Coast. It was going to be a busy summer for Jenny, too – lecture tours in Norway, Greece, France and Spain – and she was beginning to panic: about the effect her son's new interest would have on his future; about what he would do with his free time; about where she would find a nanny as reliable and inspirational as Gaynor. But, during a conversation with my parents at a friend's fiftieth birthday party, a strange idea had popped into her head – a long shot, which wouldn't solve all her problems, but which might just work.

It's always hard to work out what your parents tell their friends about your life, but you can normally guess that they make it sound considerably more interesting than it is and backdate it at least a couple of years. I couldn't tell exactly what mine had told Jenny at the party, but it had given her the idea that a) I wrote about music for a living, b) I hung out with rock stars all the time, c) I had a lot of free time this summer, d) I was desperate to take part in a road trip, and e) I was a responsible adult. What, Jenny had started to wonder, if Tom were to give Peter a kind of summer school in the realities of the rock musician's lifestyle? What if he were to take Peter around Britain, visiting landmarks and musicians, passing on his knowledge? Yes, Jenny would still have to find a new nanny, but it would take some of the pressure off her. It would also mean that Peter had someone to hang out with who was closer to his own age. Peter might be equally determined to pursue a career in music afterwards, but at least he'd have a more pragmatic, less impulsive view of his future, and plenty of ammunition to make decisions pertaining to it.

'So what do you think?' asked Jenny.

'Er . . . phew!' I said.

'I know it's a strange proposal, and I'll totally

understand if you want to say no. But er . . . don't. Please!'

The truth was, I didn't quite know *what* to say, or whether to find her belief in me flattering or misguided. In reality, I probably wasn't quite who Jenny thought I was – or at least not any more. I *had* made my living by writing about music for national newspapers for much of the previous five years, but I was in the final stages of a career change. Like many of my contemporaries who'd opted to move from music journalism to other forms of writing, I'd gradually had my soul sucked dry by the industry, until listening to new CDs and conducting thirty-minute interviews in hotel rooms were in danger of becoming what I'd never thought they would be: chores, like those you encounter in real jobs. But I wasn't kidding myself that The Man was to blame for my weariness with a career deconstructing Eminem lyrics and being horrible to The Stereophonics. The *real* blame could be assigned to three much more persuasive factors:

1. With a few rare exceptions, I only liked music made between 1957 and 1980.
2. Gigs made my ears hurt.
3. I would rather be playing golf.

These days, my music writing amounted to an article every couple of months, focusing almost exclusively on the work of someone dead with a beard who'd once been in possession of an alarmingly large collection of lutes. The last CD I had bought was Chicago's *Greatest Hits*. The only semi-famous band I had ever made friends with had stopped returning my calls after one of them was invited to appear on *Never Mind The Buzzcocks*. HMV bewildered me, MTV made me want to hide behind the sofa, excessive live music was known to give me ear infections, and the indie rock I'd bought as a teenager now sounded tuneless and I couldn't recall how or why it had ever sounded any different. I could hardly remember the last time I had stayed until the end of a gig, much less hung out backstage.

'The thing is, Jenny,' I told her, 'I love the idea in theory, but I might be a bit rubbish.'

'The thing is, Tom,' said Jenny, 'I don't mind. I'm not asking for much here. It's not that I want Peter to meet anyone really well-known or anything. Even if you were just to pass on some of your experiences, play him some records, take him to meet some of your mates – you know, even people who are involved in music in a minor way – that would be enough.

'I mean, surely you can rustle a *few* of your old contacts up? What about that bloke, the one in the photograph that your mum and dad have got? You know, the one where he's sticking his tongue in your ear.'

'Oh, Julian Cope?'

'Yeah, that's him. He'd have time to meet up with you, wouldn't he? I bet he could teach Peter a thing or two.'

I pondered this for a second. Cope, who licked his fans' ears almost as often as he modelled his hair after a root vegetable (i.e. at least three times per month), had once been the lead singer of the excellent new wave group The Teardrop Explodes, but now divided his time between writing books on Neolithic Britain, recording the occasional solo album and turning up unannounced in small villages in Wiltshire to play gigs with his novelty band, Brain Donor, while dressed in preposterously large leather boots. I thought back to the last time I'd met him: the electricity in his hand-shake, the inspiring logic at the heart of his surreal, breathless ramblings. It *had* been like meeting a real rock star, hadn't it?

I couldn't be sure that Cope would agree to meet with me. He was kind of elusive, and at one point in the mid-Eighties had locked himself in his room for several weeks, surviving only on the water biscuits his wife pushed under the door. But perhaps there were more like him out there. In fact, I knew there were. I'd met several of them over the last few years: eccentric, damaged icons, folk heroes and psychedelic loons who shunned the corporate trappings of the modern music industry, yet found their own niche within the essential musical fabric of the British Isles. I might not manage to locate many of them, and those that I did find might not fancy spending time in the company of a golf-loving Eagles fan and a bored teenager in over-sized trousers, but a sliver of hope began to emerge. Maybe I wouldn't find that elusive 'real' Britain after all, but here at least was the chance to have a lot of fun failing to do so. I tried to think of the worst thing that could happen. All I came up with was getting lost in an industrial estate in Greater Swindon. I *wanted* to get lost in an industrial estate in Greater Swindon.

'Come on, Tom,' said Jenny. 'It will be fun! Why

not come and meet him, and we'll take it from there?'

Irresistible vanity washed over me: I was going to be in charge here. This would be *my* version of a musical education. I could do this in any way I chose.

'Which day's good for you two, then?' I said.

One factor I hadn't really stopped to consider was Peter himself. What were fourteen-year-olds like these days? Moreover, what were *teenagers* like? It was only seven years since I'd been one, yet it struck me, somewhat frighteningly, that I seemed to have entirely forgotten what it was like. Now, when I thought of adolescents, I thought of the pavement outside the London Astoria in the build-up to a nu-metal gig: the pseudo-threatening band names . . . my inadvertent need to cross to the opposite side of the road . . . the accoutrements of a new kind of hollow-eyed corporate rebellion . . . the cries of 'Nigel, where's Jasmine? She's got my System Of A Down t-shirt!'

I'd found teenagers scary and slightly confusing when I was one myself; now I just found them perplexing and unsavoury. I did my best to live and shop in places where they didn't, and generally avoided them in the street, half-convinced that they were either going to ask me to give them a counselling session or beat me up for looking at their 'bird'. Earlier in the year, a national newspaper had commissioned me to write a feature which involved manufacturing my own boy band. My editor had instructed me to head out on to the streets of the capital to recruit 'talent' between the ages of fifteen and eighteen, but I'd spent the afternoon browsing in second-hand bookshops instead. In the end, my band, Boyzcout, had been constructed out of a group of friends in their mid-twenties, all of whom, after the influence of make-up, had the common trait of looking twenty-four instead of twenty-seven. We'd tried hard to pack plenty of *NSync harmonies and hip, modern references to text-messaging and the dot com world into our single, 'Zcouting For Boyz' – 'I'll zcout for you babe while we're out zcouting for boys' – but record company A&R men had rejected the demo for being too mature. 'It's a bit like *Mojo* magazine in musical form,' said one.

I knew I was turning into an old fart, perhaps prematurely, but I didn't care. There was no shame in my love of The Eagles, Journey's 'Don't Stop Believing', fuzzy dressing gowns, Sainsbury's Taste The Difference range, weak beer, golf and the VH1 Classic Rock channel; just lots of self-righteous enjoyment. I'd spent the previous seven years becoming increasingly scornful of my former self. I'd sold his records, taken the piss out of his hairstyle and mercilessly mocked his tactics with women. Occasionally I felt the odd bit of reluctant affection for him, of course, but ultimately I thought he was a wally – although I certainly believed his spiritual descendants to be a thousand times worse.

I was fully aware that it was a cliché to feel like your generation had made better things of their youth than the generation that followed, but that didn't stop me feeling the same thing with every fibre of my being. To put it bluntly, today's teens repelled me. I didn't like their grunting, complaining music, I didn't like their shapeless clothes, I didn't like the prongs of gel-plastered hair on their fringes, I didn't like their baseball caps, I didn't like the big speakers in their cars, I didn't like their piercings and I didn't like the way they hassled me for bus fares in the market square of my home town. And, from the little bits of evidence I could gather, they probably weren't gagging to add me to their speed dial either. When I had tried to convey my honest sentiments about youth trends such as nu-metal, skateboarding and gangsta rap in a newspaper article, I'd inevitably received an angry letter in response from a frustrated sixteen-year-old with a name like Toad or Jemima, lambasting me for a) my lack of understanding of the isolation the modern adolescent feels, and b) my lack of comprehension about why Slutbone or Composition Of A Horse had to insert the word 'plasma' into every second verse of their lyrics. This, naturally, had the effect of making me feel even more righteous.

Peter was an anomaly in that he didn't fit into either of the categories in which I'd come to place teens: he didn't remind me distastefully of the old version of me, but he didn't remind me distastefully of the people I used to have fights with at school either. From our initial, fleeting encounter, I'd worked out several things about him: that he was tall for his age, that he was considerably better educated than I had been at his age, that black was his favourite colour, that he was uncomfortable with his hair, and that he had watched the Oliver Stone biopic *The Doors* at some point in the previous twenty-four hours. He was the essence of sub-Jim Morrison hangdog adolescence, yet he was something alien to me, too – a kind of teenager that I'd never been in a position to have to understand. Jenny might have been friends with my parents from her student days, but while they still lived in a cosmopolitan enough area of North Nottinghamshire, she had long ago moved to a subregion of North London where it was possible to buy a jar of pimento-stuffed olives from any one of seven local outlets at three o'clock in the morning. She'd sent Peter to the local independent school, where, among the children of art gallery owners, daytime TV presenters and pop stars, he was groovily encouraged to learn in the direction that he wanted to learn. Having been to a comprehensive school whose twin areas of progressive excellence were football and beating the living crap out of the year below you, I didn't quite comprehend what this style of education involved, but I was almost certain that it meant Peter knew a lot bigger words than I'd known at his age, and probably a few bigger ones than I knew now.

Would we get on? Did Peter have any enthusiasm for the project, or did he just see it as something his mum had pushed him into? It was far too early to tell. By the end of Peter's first encounter with me, his only gestures of communication had been 'Mmmmawwwrighttt' and 'Yeah, s'even better than *Back In Black*.' Jenny, ever helpful, had assured me that in normal English this translated, respectively, as 'Hello! You must be Tom, the music writer who is going to help me further my development and learn about multifarious aspects of our musical heritage!' and 'I'm so glad we both like the work of AC/DC! I think this provides an indication that we're going to get along just spiffingly!', but I wasn't so confident. It occurred to me that, as a premature fogey, I'd spent my whole adult life hanging around with people older than me, people who treated me as their equal but always with the unspoken agreement that I was their apprentice. It didn't matter how many Hall And Oates albums I bought; providing my mates were older than me, I would always feel slightly wet behind the ears. Now the situation was reversed. I was about to spend six months feeling old for the first time in my life, and I wasn't sure I liked the idea. My parents, who had both made a living as teachers while I was growing up, had warned me from an early age not to follow their career path, and I wondered if I was about to find out why. Sure, moulding Peter in my image would be a great way to get my own back on a generation that got on my nerves, but I could see, from five minutes in his company, that there would be minimal effort on his part. He wasn't going to make me feel like he was the least bit interested in me, my life or my friends. And I would have to learn a whole new way of speaking and acting: patient, cool, encouraging, effervescent, selfless, yet somehow disciplined and slyly exemplary.

In the week that preceded my first official journey with Peter, Jenny and I began to draw up an itinerary for the summer. Due to Peter's school commitments, this would be no ordinary road trip: it would take place in carefully planned stages, featuring minimal late nights and plenty of wholesome food. Long journeys might be a problem, particularly on school nights, as would the distance between my house, in Norfolk, and Jenny's, in Crouch End. I started to wonder just how much time I would be spending on the London Orbital and what I would do to relieve the boredom. So much, I thought, for my loose, free-livin' road trip, where every day was a magical mystery tour.

I began to make lists of people Peter could hook up with, but always in the sceptical knowledge that rock stars are an awkward bunch and getting them in the same place at the same time as a recalcitrant adolescent might be a task no less arduous than persuading your favourite fragmented musical casualties to reunite and perform at your birthday party. In my planning I leaned heavily towards mates of mates and the kind of real people who'd be generous with their wisdom, and tried to ignore the more famous, plastic ones who might, if we were lucky, grant us twenty-five minutes of platitudes in a hotel room with their press agent eavesdropping outside the door. I could guarantee that *someone* out there would want to talk to us. What I couldn't guarantee was structure, or that Peter would become a more rounded person as a result. Jenny explained again that she simply wanted Peter 'to get more ammunition to enable him to make the right decision about his future, and to fill his spare time with something that wasn't computer games'. Was it just British music she wanted me to teach him about? 'No. Not really. Anything.' Did she want me to persuade him that he *didn't* want a career as a musician? 'No. I just want him to be sure of what he's getting himself into.' The problem was, I wasn't sure that *I* knew what he would be getting himself into. I wasn't even sure whether the people I was taking him to meet would know what *they'd* got themselves into. That was the point of rock and roll, surely: it wasn't supposed to be a carefully planned career choice.

Gradually, reality was beginning to replace my Thunderbolt and Lightfoot fantasy. Originally, I'd thought only of the *concept* of me teaching a teenager the laws of rock and roll on the road, as if the whole thing was nothing more than a movie, a series of easy-to-swallow images spliced together by Steven Spielberg for popular consumption: Peter and me in the car, arguing over a late-Sixties folk album; Peter and me being taken to an archaeological site by Julian Cope; Peter and me getting lost in Runcorn.

Well, okay. Maybe not Steven Spielberg.

The point was, this was going to be nowhere near as easy as I'd thought. Looking at the coming months with a clear head, the chances seemed slim that I would be picking up random hitch-hikers and playing surreal practical jokes at traffic lights. What had seemed like a great opportunity to be even less responsible than normal was suddenly looking like the most responsible thing I'd ever had to do. I wasn't going to be spending countless hours sitting next to a caricature of a teenager; I was going to be sitting next to the real thing, with all the messy eating habits, imbalanced taste and raging angst that that implied. I was devoting the best part of my summer to this, I realised, as I set off home from Jenny's place. I'd gone past the stage where it was going to be possible to back out. What was more, in all my meditating I'd forgotten to circumnavigate the roadworks on the North Circular, and was bringing up the rear in the South East's most monotonous traffic jam.

Not every great road movie starts with a bang, does it? I thought back to the sleepy opening frames of Seventies films like *Vanishing Point* and *Badlands*: nothing events in no-horse towns with negligible hints of the mayhem to follow. Besides, who said I was at the start? The real beginning could come at any moment I wanted it to, in virtually any setting. I was director, writer, producer and cinematographer here. There was scope for freedom, anarchy and adventure in this project, after all – it was simply a matter of loosening up, using my imagination and letting it happen. Liberated by this thought, I clicked *The Best Of The Steve Miller Band* satisfyingly into the tape machine, pushed the gear-stick back into neutral for the ninth time in as many minutes, and turned my attention to the evening's shopping list.

EDUCATING PETER

CASH OR EXCHANGE?

Before I got to know Peter, I got to know his self-image. In the prelude to our first meeting, Jenny, rather slyly, had loaned me one of his most treasured possessions: a dog-eared sketchbook. 'Just to give you an idea of the way his mind works.'

The sketchbook's cover displayed no name or tutor group, just a sticker featuring the logo for the veteran heavy metal band Metallica, as if that said all there was to say. That night, back at home after our initial meeting, I leafed through it, feeling somewhat guilt-ridden. The opening few pages largely consisted of crayon copies of band logos – AC/DC, Slipknot, The Deftones – but about halfway in I found a self-portrait of Peter, dressed in the longest jacket it's possible to wear without tripping over, strumming on a Gibson SG Standard guitar. There were certain similarities between this picture and the Peter I'd seen earlier in the evening, but differences, too. Like Real Peter, Crayon Peter dressed all in black, played guitar and wore his love of the darker end of rock and roll on his t-shirt. But while Real Peter played bass guitar, Crayon Peter played rhythm. While Real Peter's hair was brunette, awkwardly jaw-length and curly, Crayon's was jet black, shoulder-length and straight. Crayon Peter looked genuinely deep and mysterious, while Real Peter merely looked moody and worried. Crayon's clothes hung on him like the armour of a gothic warlord, while Real Peter's threatened to swallow him up. All in all, you might have said it was a pretty good likeness, if you'd either a) recently had to cancel an operation to remove a cataract, or b) seen teenage self-portraits before.

Still, since my first engagement with Peter had been so fleeting, it was the image of Crayon Peter – or Thardoz, Lord Of Goth, as I'd come to think of him – that I carried with me in my mind as I readied myself for our maiden voyage. The only person who wore black on a permanent basis for whom I'd ever had any respect was the South African golf legend Gary Player, but unaccountably I found myself wanting to impress Thardoz. How could I win his trust? What would he think of my collection of brightly coloured shirts, flares and Fleetwood Mac t-shirts? What would his feeling be towards 'Lollipop Years: 1967–73', the self-made, sunshine-themed compilation tape I currently had on permanent rotation in the car stereo? How would this Satan-worshipping Brandon Lee-lookalike react when the chirpy opening chords of 'Goody Goody Gumdrops' by the 1910 Fruitgum Company kicked in?

Moreover, what about the car itself? I'd never seen a

Ford Fiesta in a road movie. Scratch that: I'd never seen a Ford Fiesta in a *movie*. It was a car synonymous with the quotidian, an automobile almost indelibly linked with the phrase 'I'm just nipping down the road to Tesco – would you like me to get any celery?' Recently, I'd been slowly coming to terms not only with its unsuitability to a road trip environment, but its unsuitability to the lifestyle of a vaguely upwardly mobile man of twenty-seven. Something had finally clicked when, during a job for a sports magazine, an Audi-driving affiliate of the England cricket team had sneeringly pointed out his amazement that I had trekked the entire width of England in my 'little car'. Made in 1997, the vehicle couldn't even be written off as stylishly retro. It was just plain boring.

I was perfectly aware I needed a replacement. My problem was finding a balance between the cars of my juvenile dreams, the kind of car that Thardoz would be impressed with, and the kind of car that would demonstrate my responsible nature to Jenny. What I needed was a cross between an Aston Martin, the Batmobile and a station wagon. What I wanted was the 1968 Karman Ghia that had been sitting, unloved, outside my local used Volkswagen dealer for too long. What I *bought* was a slightly used Ford Focus estate. Sure, it was dreary and responsible, but it had one of those devices where the car stereo gets louder in tandem with the engine's revs, dictating that I could listen to 'Life In The Fast Lane' by The Eagles without the fast lane joining in on percussion. Not only that, I liked the noise that the indicator made.

'You don't want one of those classic cars, son,'

Norman, the avuncular sales assistant at Busseys, Norwich's premier Ford dealer, had advised me. 'You listen to your Uncle Norman. I've been working with Fords for forty years, and this is the best car they've made. You don't want to go messing around at those second-hand dealers. I mean, do you want to spend half your time on the hard shoulders of motorways, mending fan belts?'

'What's a fan belt?' I'd asked Uncle Norman.

Once again, when it came to the crunch, I had let down my younger self, who would almost certainly have plumped for the Karman Ghia. I felt bad about this to an extent, but that extent decreased somewhat as I realised my Ford Focus had dual beverage holders and a button which opened the boot from the interior. Besides, why should I owe my teenage self anything? Okay, so he'd done me a favour by dropping out of university after three months, but he'd worn shapeless clothes, listened to music that sounded like it had been recorded in a coal bunker, frequently chosen his friends and girlfriends badly, and made embarrassing pronouncements on the state of the universe.

That said, even if I didn't want to revisit the mindset of an early Nineties teenager, it was important that I got at least a vague insight into the thinking of his modern day equivalent. I owed Peter that much. Thus, as the day of our first expedition drew nearer, I began to venture tentatively into the unknown and research the very age group I was most afraid of: Generation Why, the even more confused and disenfranchised descendants of Generation X. From my local bookshop, I purchased *Adolescence: The Survival Guide*

For Parents And Teenagers by Elizabeth Fenwick and Dr Tony Smith, a self-help book which gave useful yet temperate suggestions on how to deal with troublesome adolescents who did things like listen to techno music at unsociable volumes and moon over pictures of Christina Aguilera. From my local video shop, I hired the first five seasons of *Buffy The Vampire Slayer*. This gave me the opportunity to relearn the rules of teenage sarcasm, along with totally new phrases like 'You're giving me the wiggins', 'No biggie', 'Cutie patootie' and 'Wipe that face off your head, bitch'. From a satellite entertainment channel, I at last found out who mysteriously ubiquitous teen icons like Freddie Prinze Jr, Heath Ledger, Kirsten Dunst and Katie Holmes were. Finally, from my local record shop, I purchased a copy of Wheatus's massive-selling single 'Teenage Dirtbag'. To my astonishment, I discovered I quite liked it – even the bit at the end where the girl who sounds like a constipated witch starts singing. These were all important initial measures, since I sensed this adventure wasn't going to be entirely about Peter's education, but mine as well.

Our opening trip was to be a three-parter, revolving loosely around the theme of Loose Cannons Of Rock: a tube journey to the Rock Circus in Piccadilly, followed by a drive to the garage on Romford Road that The Rolling Stones had been arrested for urinating against in 1965, before heading down to Hastings to meet Ed The Troubadour, one of South East England's most notorious buskers. The last leg was going to be something of a lottery. I'd never met Ed, but I'd seen him wandering around the streets of Camden Town, dressed in authentic medieval garb, playing traditional folk music and Fifties rock and roll. Rumour had it that he'd once been a protégé of Sam Phillips, the man who'd discovered Elvis, but that ever since then his career had been in freefall, resulting in violent and impulsive behaviour and a penchant for strangely coloured tights. I'd phoned Ed after acquiring his cell-phone number from an acquaintance in a country band, and a friendly voice pitched somewhere between Dennis Hopper and Eeyore from Winnie The Pooh had replied that it would be delighted to hook up. I'd been told that Ed rarely strayed beyond the thirteenth century in his fashion sense, and I thought the mobile phone seemed an incongruous auxiliary touch. Perhaps stranger still, unlike many of the other musicians I'd approached in connection with my adventure with Peter, Ed had barely needed me to explain the point of the trip before agreeing to an interview. It was as if he encountered rock journalists hanging out with adolescent friends of their family on a daily basis. How had he wound up in Hastings? I asked. 'I thought I'd follow in the footsteps of William the Conqueror,' he replied, not seeming to be taking the piss. I didn't know what to expect from Ed.

What I felt certain I *could* rely on, however, were waxworks. They had a tendency not to act too irrationally or impetuously. I'd first visited the Rock Circus, Britain's premier music-themed waxworks museum, a couple of years previously with my friend Allan. Together we'd marvelled at how closely the model of The Who's Pete Townshend resembled the former *Blue Peter* presenter Peter Duncan, rejoiced in the fact that we both had much bigger hands than Meatloaf, and insulted Michael Jackson's bum-fluff. To me, the place seemed like one of London's hidden musical treasures. With the exception of Allan, though, I was yet to meet another English-speaking, music-loving acquaintance who'd been there. This seemed somewhat sad, since to see the Circus's Bruce Springsteen model – one of the venue's few special 'animated' dolls – doing its creaky, jerking dance as it sang 'Born In The USA' was somehow to get a tiny glimpse of God. To me, the Rock Circus seemed like the ideal place to begin Peter's rock and roll journey. He wouldn't be too overawed, yet he'd also get a sense of the inherent anticlimax involved in meeting nine out of ten of one's musical idols. From my point of view, the trip would be a good fuss-free way of covering the Fame section of his training. Not only were the idols of the Rock Circus free of meddlesome managers and publicity officers, they didn't use the phrase 'It's all about the music, man' and refrained from hitting you with their guitar when you suggested their latest album was stale and corporate.

The problem with the Rock Circus is that even when it's open it looks sort of shut. You can enter the Trocadero shopping centre, pass by the picture of Lenny Kravitz, traipse up the broken escalator, and still get the sense that you're somewhere you shouldn't be: the set, perhaps, of an Eighties horror film where dolls come to life and sing Cher's 'The Shoop Shoop Song' until you die of tedium. The result of this is that when it's *really* closed – closed for ever, even – the diehard patron is left in a kind of denial, pushing past the No-Entry cones and the 'Sorry – The Rock Circus Has Closed Down' sign, through the darkened foyer, and peering through the window, convinced that somewhere in the gloom, good ol' Bruce is still singing about blue-collar America and bopping in the way that Bernie from *Weekend At Bernie's* might if you put him under the grill for a few minutes.

'No. I think it's definitely locked,' said Peter, as I shook the door handle for the fourteenth time.

'But it can't be,' I said.

'I think it is.'

'I'm really sorry about this. I should have phoned beforehand and checked it was open.'

'Doesn't matter.'

I'd been prepared for let-downs: on the ladder of reliability, musicians, as a breed, slotted somewhere between pet cats and plumbers. But I'd imagined I could bank on the Rock Circus and its host of stars to be there for me. Somehow the closure didn't seem momentous enough. Why hadn't anyone told me about it before? Shouldn't I have heard something on the national news? More to the point, how would hundreds of Spanish tourists fill their vacations now? Had anyone considered that?

It wasn't the ideal start, but, for his part, Peter seemed to take the setback manfully. So far, I had to admit I was impressed: while not exactly forthcoming, he was nowhere near as moody or miserable as I'd imagined. And as we tramped back towards Soho, I discovered it was me, not him, who was in a despairing sulk, coming to terms with the immutable fact that there really is no truly fulfilling replacement for an afternoon spent comparing hand sizes with the guitarists from Kiss.

'I really don't mind, you know,' said Peter.

'Are you sure?' I asked.

'Totally.'

'So what do you want to do now?'

'Don't mind.'

'What about we go second-hand record shopping?'

'Alright.'

'Oh, no, actually, I've just remembered – there's a pool of killer sharks just around this corner, swimming with a random selection of 1980s children's TV presenters. It costs £2.17 to join in. How about we do that instead?'

'Don't mind.'

Okay, so I made the last part of that conversation up. Nevertheless, I was beginning to realise that it didn't matter what I suggested – there was an odds-on chance Peter would say 'alright' or 'don't mind'. Whether this was because he was being polite or because he was the most reserved adolescent in Britain, I couldn't yet tell. I imagined, though, that he would enjoy second-hand record shopping. He was, after all, male, mad on music, and – surely, merely by being a teenager – keen to impress his peers with his knowledge of cool and obscure bands. Besides, everyone enjoys second-hand record shopping, don't they?

I'm loath to count the number of hours I've spent in second-hand record shops in the last decade, but I think I can be pretty certain that I've used up more time fondling classic vinyl than I have listening to it.

For years and years, while other, more sensible rock writers sold their unwanted promotional CDs to pay for things like alcohol and council tax, I traded mine in for older, smellier records. No mountain of dusty country rock, funk or psychedelia was high enough. No musty backstreet junk shop was cunningly hidden enough: I would find it, just on the off-chance that someone had sold that elusive second Rare Earth album or Jimmy Webb promo there recently. Writing the whole pursuit off as 'work-related revision' merely allowed it to get more out of hand, until finally I found myself in a desperate state, making pathetic attempts to befriend carpenters who might be kind enough to build a contraption monolithic and elaborate enough to house my record collection.

Then, one day not too long ago, the madness stopped – not exactly abruptly, but nevertheless surprisingly quickly. The trigger could have been my mother-in-law-to-be arriving at my flat for the first time, surveying my record collection and announcing, 'You're going to *die* before you've listened to all these!' Or it could simply have been that the portion of my brain devoted to memorising esoteric early Seventies power-pop finally became overloaded and shut down in protest. Whatever the case, it dawned on me that I no longer wanted to spend every bit of spare cash I had on early Rain Parade albums that I would never listen to, nor every bit of spare time being casually insulted by men in Mogwai t-shirts. I'd always known that second-hand record shops were rancid places staffed by surly snobs. The difference was, now, for the first time, it bothered me. It seemed nicer to shop in hygienic places, with products that didn't have globules of treacle stuck to them in memory of a previous owner.

I continued to cherish vinyl, but on a more selective and casual basis, without being averse to selling the odd mound of it in order to fund a new dishwasher or pitching wedge. I still visited second-hand record shops, but more out of habit than anything. That said, the idea of going to a few of them with Peter lifted me out of my mid-afternoon slump. Here, a mischievous part of my subconscious realised, was the chance to start all over again, to rediscover the buzz of the nascent collector, albeit vicariously. Sure, *I* had an original copy of the second Matthews Southern Comfort album, but I could be pretty certain that Peter didn't, and I was excited for him because of it. Obviously, there was always the chance that he wouldn't want one – from the brief time I'd spent with him, he didn't seem like a whimsy and sideburns kind of kid – and would rather spend his money on a Marilyn Manson import, but surely, as his designated tutor and tastemaker, I was holding the cards here.

In fact, what I *was* holding wasn't like card at all; it was more like Monopoly money. The flimsy notes that I rustled together in my hand represented the special currency you received from the chain of Music And Video Exchange shops when you sold records to them and didn't want to feel like you'd got a really rotten deal. The fact that I was in possession of them was perhaps testament to the fact that I wasn't a fully recovered vinyl junkie: it meant that at some point in the last few weeks I'd sold some CDs to the Music And

Video Exchange and, upon being asked, 'Cash or exchange?', I'd opted for 'exchange', under no illusions that that 'exchange' could mean anything other than 'more records'. The problem was, 'exchange' always amounted to around twice as much as 'cash', and it was all too easy to give in to temptation.

The Music And Video Exchange shops in London are like most second-hand shops, only more so in every way. That is to say, they are packed with more records, more tetchy sales assistants, more failed musicians and more of an ambience of pseudo élitism per square yard. Unfortunately, they are also packed with potential bargains, and are quite possibly the only record shops in London which you can guarantee will take all of your unwanted CDs. While I realised the psychological risks involved in introducing a wide-eyed minor to this kind of atmosphere, I also knew that it was important to show Peter the bizarre subculture of the Music And Video Exchange, which, in its own way, formed a necessary chunk of the underbelly of the music business.

'Once we step through these doors, the etiquette of the outside world becomes irrelevant,' I explained, as we arrived outside the Soho branch of the franchise. 'Now, just act cool, and if the men inside are rude to you, don't let them see that you're bothered.'

'Alright,' said Peter.

Beyond the threshold, a typical scene emerged: knowingly uninterested sales assistants listlessly checked the condition of vinyl and made arch comments about the noise coming from the speakers – from what I could gather, a man wailing about the time another man stole his girlfriend, with some kitchen utensils falling out of a window taking the place of what traditionally would be called 'a rhythm section' – while a selection of Japanese girls with rucksacks and inventively shaved men with National Health specs rooted through the racks in the middle of the floor. I watched as Peter took it in. He seemed to be coping. Gradually we dispersed, me towards the section marked 'Prog/Psychedelia' and Peter towards a CD sleeve featuring what appeared to be – and there really was no way of getting around this, no matter which angle you chose to look at it – a ghost swallowing a human kidney.

Twenty minutes later, we reconvened, Peter clutching five or six CDs – none of which, to my relief, seemed to feature a sleeve depicting an organ-munching spectre.

'What have you found?' I asked him.

'First Marilyn Manson album. New Linkin Park. Couple of other things,' said Peter.

'Have you ever heard of these guys?' I passed him the copy of Blue Oyster Cult's classic 1976 album *Agents Of Fortune* that I'd found a few moments earlier in the Hard Rock section.

'No. Never.'

'They sound a bit like the stuff you listen to. This is their best album. You should check it out.'

'Alright.'

I was aware that I'd told a white lie: Seventies albums by Blue Oyster Cult, though squarely established in the metal genre, didn't really sound a bit like the stuff Peter listened to; they sounded like The Byrds

being kneed where it hurts by a large gang of Hell's
Angels. But my heart was in the right place. Peter was
about to face the most difficult test of the day – the
most difficult test, possibly, of his whole musical
apprenticeship – and, though ultimately he would
have to face it alone, I felt it was the least I could do to
make sure he was adequately prepared. If my planning
had been better, if the Rock Circus hadn't closed
down, I'm sure I would have saved this test for later in
our adventure, when Peter was more cynical, more
inured to the ways of men who've seen their musical
dreams slowly disintegrate before their eyes. But there
seemed to be no avoiding it. Only one thing was
certain: when it was over, he wouldn't be quite the
same person that he'd been before. Stronger, yes, but
weaker too, and never quite able to feel so optimistic
about the destiny of humanity. Following in the footsteps of heroes, Japanese rock chicks and overgrown
students, Peter was about to face one of the toughest
tests known to man: he was about to pay for some
goods at the Music And Video Exchange.

As I'd learned to my cost over the years, conducting
cash transactions at the MVE could not be approached
in the same flippant, absent-minded manner as conducting cash transactions in ordinary high street
establishments. There were rules, and then, hidden
between the lines of those, a myriad codes and sub-
clauses. If, for example, you happened to be selling
records, what you didn't do was approach the cash
register brightly and say, 'Good day to you! I've got
some goods I'd like to sell! I think you'll find they're
all in wonderful condition, particularly the copy of the

first Climie Fisher single. By the way, could you tell me the way to the nearest Virgin Megastore?' What you *did* do was look the sales assistant in the eye, grunt, shove your records across the counter in his general direction, accidentally-on-purpose knocking his coffee over in the process, then look insouciantly in the opposite direction while picking something imaginary out of your ear. But even that wouldn't necessarily see you through unscathed. This wasn't just about grunting and looking uninterested, this was about being *totally* belligerent throughout the grunt, being *utterly* committed to your uninterest as the sales assistant – a whippety man usually, giving the impression of swarthiness without being able to grow anything remotely approaching a full beard – sorted through your pile of albums and rolled his eyes at your taste as if it represented your personality in its entirety.

Buying is easier, but not much, as my friend John once found to his cost when he asked if an MVE employee would like 'the correct change', only to have a toy plastic skull placed silently in front of him in response. John never found out what this gesture meant – was it MVE code for 'No, it's okay, we've got plenty of change – look, we've even used it to buy this toy plastic skull – but thanks for asking anyway'? – but has never made the mistake of adopting a cheery, polite demeanour inside the shop since. In the Music And Video Exchange, the phrase 'Smile and the world smiles with you' is turned inside out, becoming 'Grunt in a pissed-off fashion and the world gives you grudging respect'. Besides smiling, other inadvisable things to do in an MVE include:

1. Asking for the new Chris Rea album.
2. Moshing joyously when you hear a song you get pleasure from on the shop stereo.
3. Reading a slogan on a sales assistant's t-shirt – e.g. 'Virgin Slug Weasel' – and taking it literally, then offering to help.
4. Using your real address when signing for the goods you have sold, if you live in a house called Tweedle Cottage.
5. Complaining about the volume of the music on the shop stereo and loudly observing that it sounds like some kitchen utensils falling out of a window.

Besides grunting, other advisable things to do in an MVE include:

1. Yawning.
2. Making up bands with ridiculous names – e.g. Hairshit, Top Radish, Smell Assignment – and asking the sales assistants if they've heard their new album.
3. Nodding thoughtfully when you hear a song you enjoy on the shop stereo, conveying the impression that you are not simply enjoying the music but disassembling its existential meaning.
4. Saying 'safe' a lot, repeating the word 'yeah' several times as a form of approval, and walking as if you live in downtown Compton and have recently been shot twice, as opposed to as if you live in Ladbroke Grove and have just had a takeaway patty that has upset your stomach slightly.
5. Making up a cool address – e.g. Flat 3, Snot Slum, Wandsworth – when signing for the goods you have sold.

Another excellent tactic is eclecticism. Ultimately, it's as easy to impress the Music And Video clique with your hip taste as it is to incite their ridicule with your unhip taste. Moreover, by buying the records the sales assistants consider worthy, you're merely pandering to them and confirming their belief that your life's ambition is to one day be as stylish, intellectual and credible as they are. A better option is to baffle them with your diversity – not the kind of diversity preached by pretentious people who make a point of reminding the world about how eclectic they are on a daily basis, but *real* diversity: an original twelve-inch of Robert Palmer's 'Addicted To Love', say, secreted in a pile containing the first album by the Seventies psychedelic folk group The Trees, the final four Steppenwolf albums and Living In A Box's *Greatest Hits*. This will have the effect of making their heads spin and their bottom lips wobble as they strive to remain imperturbable while quickly calculating how this pile of records fits into their tapered ideas about musical good and evil.

Peter's selection was far more simple. Coming from a fourteen-year-old, a Living In A Box/Steppenwolf combination might have smacked of sheer naivety. However, the unusual juxtaposition of Blue Oyster Cult (uncool, but not outrageously so, and something of an enigma) and nu-metal (cool, but kind of for kids) would spread just the right level of subtle confusion.

Like a worried father seeing his son through the gates on the first day of school, I watched as my young friend approached the counter, then, from a safe distance, did my best to pick up on snatches of the conversation. It's difficult, eavesdropping on a teenager and a record shop employee from six yards away, since there's no real telling if words like 'mmff-fuuh', 'd'njjj' and 'smrrright' are real words you've misheard or bona fide snatches of an alien – but, in Soho, widely recognised – form of communication. Whatever the case, I took it as a good sign that Peter hadn't burst into tears by the time he received his change.

'How did that go?' I asked him as we walked up Berwick Street towards Oxford Street a few moments later.

'Fine,' said Peter.

'What? You mean nobody put a plastic skull in front of you?'

'No. Seemed like alright blokes, really.'

'Are you sure? They're normally dead rude to me. What were you talking about to them? You seemed to take quite a while.'

'Oh, the bloke with the big stress patches on his beard and the "Patrick Moore Is My Whore" t-shirt was talking to me about this album that I bought by Kitty. He says they're playing tonight at the London Astoria.'

I was baffled, and not just because I didn't know who Kitty were. It had taken me and my friends years of training to build up psychological armour tough enough to enable us to deal with the Music And Video Exchange in-crowd, and now Peter was not only speaking their language but getting invited to gigs with them. Of course, most music-obsessed men tend to have a mental age of fourteen, so perhaps I shouldn't have found this camaraderie so surprising, but I couldn't help feeling hurt. Peter hadn't talked to *me* about Kitty. He hadn't talked much at all, really, unless I'd spoken to him first. I wasn't even sure he thought I was 'an alright bloke'.

Later, while Peter nipped off to the lavatory in Burger King, I furtively consulted *Adolescence: The Survival Guide For Parents And Teenagers*. It seemed to contain plenty of advice for adults trying to communicate with sarcastic, unsociable and bullying adolescents, but little on recalcitrance, or at least Peter's specific mode of it. Frantically, I searched for a chapter headed 'Generally Pleasant Yet Unforthcoming Teenage Acquaintances: Getting Them To Talk To You A Bit More About Rock And Stuff'. The most relevant thing I found was a section on shyness.

'Don't force painfully shy youngsters into the limelight,' advised Elizabeth Fenwick and Dr Tony Smith, 'or draw too much attention to them . . . [But] don't let them off the hook completely.' And, slightly later: 'Eating together straightaway normally helps.'

I closed the book, anticipating Peter's return. Perhaps I was expecting too much too quickly and bombarding my companion slightly. I had, after all, only met him properly for the first time four hours ago. I'd already asked him questions some of his best friends probably hadn't asked him: what were his favourite bands?, what exactly did progressive schooling entail?, was he dating anyone at the moment?, did those metal chains he had hanging off his trousers ever get snagged up embarrassingly on road bollards and tube train barriers?, why was Limp Bizkit's lead singer on the executive board at East West records? It was hardly surprising that most of the answers I'd received were monosyllabic. We hadn't even had a meal together yet.

As we tucked into our bacon double cheeseburgers, I resolved to cool my approach slightly, and almost immediately – whether as a direct result of this, by sheer coincidence, or because I was sneakily allowing him to break Jenny's No-Fast-Food rule – Peter started to open up. For the first time he began to talk of Raf, one of his friends at school, who had 'the coolest leather jacket' and could play the whole of Nirvana's *Nevermind* album on guitar. Peter liked *Nevermind*? But that was from *my* era. 'Yeah,' he said, 'so?' He liked it a lot – had done before anyone else in his school year. He and his mates were always listening to it; his band, Goat Punishment, liked to cover a couple of songs from it. Peter had a band? Of *course* he had a band. What did I think – that he played the guitar just for the sake of it? In fact, he had two bands, although the other one, Toast Hero, was 'just a side project'.

'Goat Punishment are called Goat Punishment because in the quadrangle at school there's a pen with goats in it.'

'And you want to punish them?'

'No. We like them. It's just a name. Adam, our drummer, wanted us to be called The Fuckers, originally.'

'But that's a bit rubbish, isn't it?'

'Yeah. The rest of us thought so.'

It made no odds that Peter was growing up in an

environment that bore almost no resemblance to the one in which I had spent my teenage years: the protocol of communication was exactly the same. Here, you didn't get what you gave; you got what you didn't give. If Peter and I were going to get on, I would have to fight my urge to fill every moment of silence with inane jabber and interrogative angling. Worryingly quickly, I found myself back in a bastardised version of my 1989 mindset – desperate to impress the cool kids, but trying to hold back my natural tendency towards politeness and inquisitive-ness, in the knowledge that I'd be liked a lot less for what I did say than what I didn't. The bacon double cheeseburger didn't help. I was fourteen again, and all that was missing were the Mr Whippy hairstyle, the Campri ski jacket and the Cathy Dennis poster.

Was Peter a cool kid? I'd originally assumed not. Now I wasn't so sure. True, he had disobedient hair, a little acne, a lot of black clothes and a few obvious social problems, but, while those attributes might have lost him a few friends in the adult universe, there was no telling where it put him on the ladder of adolescent popularity. I reminded myself of his age: fourteen, not seventeen. I looked at his clothes: Doc Martens, leather trenchcoat, AC/DC t-shirt, that metal chain thing that I still didn't understand. Did anyone I'd known at fourteen dress like this out of school hours? Highly unlikely. They probably wouldn't have wanted to in an era when Patrick Swayze was considered a fashion icon, but that was beside the point. The point was that this was a pretty advanced look for a fourteen-year-old. At least, I supposed it was. I didn't know for sure.

I'd spent most of the last seven years ignoring teenagers, remember?

Hiking up Crouch Hill back to the car with Peter dragging a few paces behind me, kicking gravel, I told myself to snap out of it. I was a married man with a Ford Focus, life assurance and a perfectly nice group of regular friends. I wasn't here to impress my teenage companion, or even to become his pal; I was here to give him a lesson in the ways of rock, plain and simple. If we bonded in the process, fine. If we didn't, my life would not be significantly altered.

That said, it was going to make for some mighty awkward car journeys.

EDUCATING PETER

LET IT TRICKLE

The story, as it's traditionally told, begins with a Daimler pulling into a garage forecourt. Eight or nine young men and women emerge boisterously from the car. One of them asks to use the lavatory. The petrol station's resident mechanic, who's come out to see what the commotion is, says no, he won't allow it. Slowly, the gang break into a chant of 'We'll piss anywhere, man!', as two of the men – one of particularly memorable appearance due to the size of his lips – urinate against the petrol station wall. The group get back in the car and it pulls away with, according to the *Daily Express*, 'the people inside sticking their hands through the window in a well-known gesture' (it being 1965, you assume this gesture involves double digits as opposed to the later, somehow less swashbuckling 'flipped bird'). The police are alerted. Three of the agitators are fined five pounds.

It's not, it has to be said, the most scandalous tale of rock and roll hell-raising ever told. Next to, for example, the story about the Led Zeppelin groupie and the red snapper or Keith Moon driving his Rolls-Royce into a swimming pool, you might even say it was a little on the sissy side. These days, the Shell station on the Romford Road doesn't have a mechanic, but if it did, you suspect that, were you to piss against his wall, he'd barely look up from his copy of the *News Of The World*, where there would be every chance he'd be reading about celebrities who indulged in far more licentious activities than urinating in public. In place of that original mechanic were a couple of downcast Asian men in their mid-twenties, selling petrol, fags and, just occasionally, disposable cameras from behind the safety of a Plexiglas partition. Their generation would still know of the miscreant with the prominent lips, but less because of his music and more because of the frequent stories in the tabloids about his philandering with Latin women young enough to be his daughter.

'Sorry to bother you,' I said to one of them (the men selling petrol, not the Latin women) as I handed over the money for a disposable camera, 'but you wouldn't happen to know if this is the garage which the Rolling Stones urinated against in 1965, would you?'

Peter lurked behind me, flicking through a copy of *Kerrang!*

The men who work at the Shell station on Romford Road get asked about pissing a lot. At first they look at you suspiciously, as if merely by being in this dodgy corner of London and wanting to make conversation you must be up to no good. But then their tight scowls break into voluptuous grins and they point you towards the legendary spot, chuckling.

Did they think that the mythical value of their bricks gave them an edge over the Esso station across the road, which only has a normal, prosaic wall? I wondered.

'Perhaps.' They laughed.

'Has anyone ever thought of erecting a plaque?'

'Oh, no. I don't think Mr Shell would like that!'

'And what about The Stones? Do they come back here much?'

'Not really.'

'What about other bands? Do they like to piss here, too? You know, like the way dogs like to piss where other dogs have pissed.'

'Er. Mmm. No.'

I'd always loved The Rolling Stones – thought of them, perhaps, as the ultimate band – and felt that I'd be a pretty lame teacher if I couldn't find a valuable lesson for my pupil somewhere within their four-decade history. Romford Road seemed a good place to start, since a) Mick Jagger was too busy promoting his latest movie venture to show us around his mansion, b) it was one of the few legendary spots associated with the group that didn't charge an entry fee, and c) it was on the way to Brighton, where we were scheduled to stay at my in-laws' house, before dropping in on Ed The Troubadour in Hastings the following day. I also had a vague memory of a student teacher once using a poem about people pissing on the floor as a disarming device on my fourth-year English class. 'The Waz' might have been a hackneyed con-versation loosener between adults and children, but that didn't mean I wasn't going to use it to my full advantage.

My original intention had been for Peter and me to recreate the famous piss, but as the day had gone on, I'd become more and more worried about stage fright. Besides, now we'd befriended the petrol station's employees, being rude to them and provoking them to call the police was going to be slightly less practical, especially as I'd asked one of them to take a photograph on our behalf. So, instead, we hunched over and mimed the crime, looking back over our shoulder and scowling like Satanic Majesties as the cash assistant shouted 'Cheese!' What can I say? It was tacky. It was touristy. It was precisely the sort of thing I'd hoped we'd get up to on our adventure.

For the first time, Peter seemed to be enjoying himself. Fortified by the family-sized pack of Wheat Crunchies I'd bought him at the Crouch End branch of Budgens, he'd begun to open up and relax on the way here, even going as far as to tell a few anecdotes, almost all of which would start with the phrase 'It was really funny . . .' and involve one of his friends putting a pair of pants on their head. Still, I couldn't help puzzling over what he really thought of the latest stage of his musical education. To me, The Rolling Stones were still untouchably insouciant icons, but that was because I owned twenty-one of their albums and had spent a third of my life pretending I was living in a late-Sixties utopia. To most of my generation, they were shrivelled old skinflints. To Peter's generation – or at least the members of it that had bothered to notice the second biggest band in the history of the universe existed – they were probably something much more decrepit and embarrassing.

'You've heard of Mick Jagger, right?' I'd asked Peter earlier, in the car.

'Yeah. Of course. He's the one who tries to pretend to be young by shagging all those women and making that sad album with those hip-hop guys. I saw that documentary about him on TV, where he was taking the piss out of Kate Winslet.'

'What about Keith Richards?'

'Think so.'

'You should do. He's the really cool one. What about Charlie Watts and Ron Wood?'

'Ummm . . . not sure.'

I decided not to mention Bill Wyman. As a rule, it's best not to. Besides, we had only just eaten.

It was one thing playing Peter The Stones' invincible 1973 album, *Exile On Main Street* (Peter: 'This is alright, actually'), going into a bookshop and showing him a picture of Keith Richards taken during the making of its predecessor, *Sticky Fingers*, and convincing him that The Stones had once been the coolest men on earth. It was another thing entirely trying to convince him that they'd been the wild men of rock as well. One of Peter's favourite bands, Slipknot, regularly defecated live on stage without being noticed, never mind arrested. Merely by opening their mouths and switching on their microphones, other groups he listened to could replicate the sensation of having someone projectile-vomit down your ear canal. Why was he going to be impressed by a group of former art students having a slash against a petrol station?

I pictured the months ahead, and wondered what kind of battle I was facing. How hard was I going to have to try to impress him? Just how anaesthetised was he to the murkiest reaches of Rock And Roll Babylon? As we stood and focused on the scene of the crime, I attempted to give him a sense of historical perspective: a 1965 world on the brink of upheaval, with flower power just around the corner, when pop music genuinely seemed dangerous. He nodded a lot – it was difficult to know if he was taking it in or not – then went to purchase two tubes of Pringles from the kiosk.

'Can you feel it in the air? The sense that you're somewhere special?' I asked him upon his return.

'I'm not sure. I'm a bit too cold to feel anything at the moment,' he said.

'But can you picture it? It was a pretty daring thing to do in 1965, you know.'

'Yeah. It sort of sounds like fun. My mate Raf's brother sometimes drives around with eight people in his car. I think you're supposed to only have five.'

'You could probably fit eight in a Daimler, though.'

'Yeah.'

'I suppose it's a good job that the car didn't cut out when they were trying to pull away. That would have ruined the moment a bit.'

'Mmm.'

With one last wistful look – well, a wistful look from me; a slightly relieved one from Peter – we turned for the Focus. It started first time. Sticking our hands out the window in a well-known gesture that the Rolling Stones probably didn't use, we waved to our new friends in the booth and pulled out into the unruly early evening traffic. It was, after all, just a wall, and there was only so long you could stare at it.

EDUCATING PETER

REALLY FUNNY

'It was really funny. There's this guy in my year, Sam, who's, like, really cool on guitar. He can play all bottleneck and stuff, but he's a bit of a mosher . . .'

'What's a mosher?'

'Well, it's kind of like a goth, but not quite.'

'What? More energetic?'

'Yeah.'

'It's weird. Moshing was just a kind of dancing you did when I was a kid; now it's a whole lifestyle choice. Bizarre. Anyway – sorry. Carry on.'

'Yeah, so Sam's like showing off in Mrs Williams' music class, playing this Feeder song, and Raf, who's in year eleven, walks in, and he's like, "What's going on?" And we're like, "Oh-oh," 'cos Raf's, like, the best guitar player in the world, ever – better than Sam. And they start having this duel, and Sam's playing this Feeder song really quick, but Raf just keeps getting quicker, and Mrs Williams walks in and she's just watching, going, "Wow." It was so cool.'

'I never really got into music lessons at school. I had a problem with those weird xylophone-type things that you had to blow into. The bit where you put your mouth always seemed to still be covered with the spit of the last person who'd used it. Do you have those?'

'Er . . . no.'

'So is Raf your best mate?'

'Yeah, probably. He's a couple of years older than me, but we've got really similar taste and stuff. He got me into Nirvana and AC/DC.'

'And he's in your band?'

'Yeah. He's in Goat Punishment. It's kind of his band, really. He writes the songs.'

'You write your own songs? That's pretty impressive.'

'We do a few covers. There's this song by American Hi-Fi that I really hate, but the rest of the band like it. We do "Lithium" by Nirvana, too.'

'It's weird that you like Nirvana, 'cos I'm – what? – thirteen years older than you, and most of the people I knew when I was growing up liked them too. I saw them play once, you know.'

'No *way*. Really?'

'Mmm. I could never really understand what all the fuss was about, to be honest. Although it was always a good excuse to push people over when they played them at my local student night.'

'I don't know. They're just really . . .'

'I always preferred Smashing Pumpkins. But I hate them now.'

'. . . intense.'

'So have you done any gigs yet?'

'Sort of, but only at school. There's this thing at school they have every month, which was called Folk Night. Last time it was really funny, 'cos there was all this mulled wine, for all the parents who had come to watch, and everyone kept stealing it, and all the glasses were shaking and stuff on the table 'cos we were playing so loud when we did "Lithium", even though it was unplugged.'

'You said it *was* called Folk Night.'

'Yeah, they changed it 'cos we complained.'

'You don't like folk?'

'Well, kind of, but it's not that. It's just not really what anyone plays.'

'So what is the night called now?'

'Axe Demons.'

EDUCATING PETER

TIGHTS

'Now. Just a warning. He's going to be coming around that corner in a minute, and he's going to be dressed slightly strangely.'

'Like, how? What do you mean, "strangely"?'

'Well, he's going to be wearing purple tights, for a start.'

'What, *just* purple tights?'

'Well, no. I imagine he'll have a kilt on as well, or an extremely long cape. Maybe a broadsword, too.'

'But how do you know his tights will be purple?'

'He just told me on the phone. That's what he said: "I'll be the one in the purple tights." '

'And what did you say?'

'I said, "Er . . . cool." What else do you say at moments like that?'

'Here he is.'

'You say, "Here he is"?'

'No. I mean, I think this is him. Look – those are quite purple.'

'Oh, right. Yeah. They are. It must be. Okay. Oh . . . *Oh*.'

EDUCATING
PETER

MR ED

There are two important things to remember when socialising in a refined coffee house in a historic coastal town with a man kitted out authentically as a member of Robin Hood's Merry Men. One: don't let him get his banjo out. And two: if he waves his axe around, cut the conversation short.

For close to twenty minutes now, I'd had one eye on the ladies sitting to the left of our table in the Hastings branch of Costa Coffee, and I'm pretty sure Peter had too. Obviously these were respectable women, perhaps in their late forties, possibly called Jan and Gloria, impeccably dressed without being showy, probably with steady, long-serving jobs in the beauty department of John Lewis or Debenhams. All they wanted, you could see, was to have a quiet mocha, compare new curtains and grouse about the respective shortcomings of their daughters' fiancés. And I had to give them credit: they were doing very well at getting on with it. But you could tell the scene to their immediate right was beginning to bother them, the little indignant explosions going off in their heads one by one: who was the bearded, grey-haired man, and why was he dressed like a Knight of the Round Table? What on earth was he doing hanging out with the younger man with the fluffy sideburns and the Fleetwood Mac t-shirt? And what relation were the two of them to the bored-looking boy with the dark clothes and the peculiar chains hanging off his trousers?

It was the axe that finally did it. In his defence, Ed wasn't intending to do any harm by unsheathing it and holding it in the air for me and Peter to see. It wasn't even a very big axe – about a foot and a half long, at the most. Nevertheless, he didn't really make any attempt to disguise it. It was clearly too much for Jan and Gloria. Grabbing their coats quickly, but making sure to straighten their chairs, they headed for the door, emitting just-audible wibbling noises.

Ed didn't even seem to notice. He was talking about tapeworm.

'Tapeworm' is what Ed The Troubadour calls the thugs who make his job a living nightmare – the people who verbally and physically abuse him while he busks, the people who set fire to his Reliant Robin shortly after he arrived in Hastings. But Tapeworm, for Ed, can also be a catch-all term for the disease of modern man. Occasionally, as he sat with Peter and me in Costa Coffee, he pointed to young men – dead-eyed young men, admittedly, but young men who ultimately looked fairly harmless – who were passing by the window. 'Look,' he muttered. 'Tapeworm. Grrr.'

For Ed, it all came down to hair. 'Everything was better before everyone started cutting their hair off,' he told us. 'People, I mean, and music. I think hair's a very spiritual thing. Now look at them all. They all look the same. Tapeworm.'

Ed told us he hadn't cut his hair since the late Sixties. He had the appearance of a silver lion. He looked good for his age (he was fifty-five), but said he didn't feel it. He felt white-hot pain throbbing from his foot, meaning he could only work for two or three hours per day. He didn't like Hastings and felt trapped: he could never make any money here, but didn't really know where else to go.

I'd interviewed quite a few buskers in the past, and most of them had heard of Ed. There were stories galore: about him busking on Christmas Day; about disturbed residents pouring buckets of water on his head; about him threatening to put superglue in the locks of the same disturbed residents' cars; about him trying to get folk bands to put him up for the night; about him turning up uninvited to the premier of a documentary about the life of Sam Phillips from Sun Records, only to be manhandled to the floor by bouncers, then rescued by the documentary's subject and lavished with a front-row seat. He was a mythical figure in country, rock and roll and folk circles: a modern-day minstrel of no fixed abode who felt that he had been fleeced when, in their search for a sound-track composer, the producers of the *Lord Of The Rings* trilogy had overlooked him in favour of Enya. My own experience of his music had been limited to two olde English ballads he'd played at Nashville

Babylon, a regular Sunday afternoon country rock get-together in Camden. Both songs had stood distinctly apart from the warped Americana that the crowd had heard from other performers that afternoon, yet in that setting the concept of Ed had seemed almost normal (he could have been dressing the way he did ironically, or for a dare, or seriously – it didn't matter; it was London). Now it seemed less normal. And Hastings quite clearly thought so.

I'd lied to Peter in the build-up to meeting Ed, giving him the impression that getting together with him would be an out-and-out fun thing, when only a small part of me believed it. A bigger part of me sensed that this would be one of the harshest parts of Peter's education – a stark lesson in the downside of the rock and roll existence. Ed's life, by all accounts, had been somewhat tragic, and rarely more so than in the last few months. In truth, I was here for two reasons: not simply on behalf of Peter, but also on behalf of Big Steve, organiser of Nashville Babylon and lead singer of the alternative country band The Arlenes, who was worried about Ed and wanted me to talk him into returning to London.

The way Ed told it, the trouble had all started towards the end of last year, when police had broken down the door of his room in the West End hostel he was staying in. Exactly why they'd broken in wasn't quite made clear – not to Peter and me, and not to Ed by the sound of it. But Ed had been thoroughly spooked. He'd packed his few possessions – tights, the armour that he'd bought from an antique clothing shop in Nottingham, the cloaks that he'd made for himself, some tapes, a dozen or so medieval weapons – into his Reliant Robin and taken off, with no aim other than to see where he ended up.

'Cool!' I enthused to Ed. 'That's kind of what me and Peter are doing. Just rolling along. Trying not to let the sound of our wheels drive us crazy.'

Ed appraised us silently, apparently not thinking it was cool at all. He continued the story.

'I slept in the car for a while,' he said. 'You'd be surprised how comfortable those things are. Then I found a place up the road from here.'

Earlier, on the phone, he had invited us up to the 'place up the road from here', and I'd politely skirted the issue. It wasn't that I didn't want to see his bedsit: I did, very much. But Ed had talked about 'snails on the floor' and 'tapeworms' living in the flat below and I was worried about Peter. Sure, I wanted to show him a heart-rending aspect of the musical existence and give him a crazy adventure, but I didn't want to scare the living daylights out of him.

I looked across at my young companion now, wondering if I'd made the right decision. He was picking at his lip, not giving the impression that he had any living daylights to scare.

Every so often, during a break in Ed's monologue, I would try to get Peter involved in the conversation, by (if Ed talked about choral music) interjecting with 'Peter's mum and dad like choral music!', or (if Ed talked about lutes) interjecting with 'Peter got taught how to play the lute at his school!' This would merely result in a small pause, or, at best, a grunt from Peter and an 'Oh' from Ed, before Ed resumed the monologue and Peter resumed playing with the small hunk of Eccles cake that was left on his plate. I was starting to get an inkling of how stepfathers feel when they're trying to get kids from separate marriages to acknowledge one another's existence. Peter was either genuinely bored or doing a great job of pretending to be nonchalant about the irregular nature of the situation. Ed's radar, meanwhile, didn't seem to pick up Peter at all. He was too busy telling his life story. Still, you couldn't really blame him: it was an interesting one.

Since he started busking in the late Sixties, Ed told us, he had performed in eleven different countries and 250 different cities. He announced, proudly, that buskers had been the Queen Mother's favourite form of entertainer. 'Some of the richest people in the world!' he said. I assumed he was talking figuratively. In the old, good days, he explained, he could easily earn £200 for a day's work, but now he was lucky if he made an eighth of that. 'Nobody cares in this place,' he lamented, gesturing towards an obese woman in a baseball cap across the road who was walking a German shepherd, as if it was all her fault. 'My foot hurts too much to do more than three or four hours at a time. And I wouldn't busk at night. Too dangerous here.' He always carries his weapons with him – a sword, a bow or an axe. 'The police have confiscated them a few times, but they've always had to give them back. It's part of ancient law, y'know: a busker is allowed to be armed.'

Ed was born in North East England but moved to Memphis in the mid-Sixties, and his drawn-out vowels reflect more of the latter. His wandering spirit had taken him from a cardboard box beneath the Brooklyn Bridge in New York all the way to the Robin Hood statue in Nottingham, which used to be one of his favourite places to play. I told him I spent the first twenty years of my life in Nottingham. 'Do you know the story from the early Nineties about the busker who split his landlord's head open with a broadsword?' he asked me. I said I vaguely remembered something of the sort. 'That was me!' he said, bristling slightly. 'He did kung-fu on me and I whacked him one. He got forty-five stitches. I got seven months in prison.' Ed talked a lot about violence – the winos who'd attacked him while he busked, the drunken townies who'd tried to steal his instruments – and seemed to feel that the modern city high street was no place to hang out unarmed.

The best period of his life was in Memphis, where he met Elvis's dad ('lovely bloke'), refinished the guitar that The King used on his '68 Comeback Tour, and, with his band The Jesters, cut some rocking demos for Sam Phillips of Sun Records. He recalled the day that Phillips asked him to sign to the label in that vivid way people reserve for the moments that have made or ruined them.

'I'd been told by a friend that I shouldn't do it, that I'd be signing my life away. I was stupid. I said no, and almost got into a punch-up with him [Phillips]. Biggest mistake of my life. Everything changed that day.' A tear came into his eye as he said it, and I thought I saw a rare flicker of emotion from Peter. It was hard to know what to say, so I offered everyone another coffee.

Earlier, before we'd settled on the coffee house as a good place to sit down, Ed had suggested we get a drink at a pub across the road from the town square, but, having entered it, he'd looked around nervously, then led us out. 'Tapeworm,' he'd hissed, by way of explanation. Throughout our encounter, he maintained a strange combination of paranoid energy and stoned lethargy, which seemed to fit quite well with the conflicting mixture of hippy philosophy and macho hostility that made up his worldview. The sad thing was, he talked a lot of sense, between the bitterness. It was hard to imagine a right place for Ed in modern Britain, but it quite clearly wasn't Hastings. Had he thought about going back to London? 'Yeah, but it's a question of getting the money together. And where would I go?' Would he think about playing at Nashville Babylon again? 'I don't know. It depends on the price. Playing for nothing – that's just a mug's game for me these days.'

It was a blustery day in Hastings, oppressed by a low grey sky, and Peter and I found ourselves wandering around the town centre in a kind of daze as morning turned into afternoon, like survivors of our own mini-earthquake. Peter looked shivery and underdressed, with just the flimsiest of AC/DC tour t-shirts under his big leather jacket. We had no real reason to stay here – the record shops catered for neither my love of adult-oriented rock nor Peter's yen for obscure Norwegian blood metal, the lone guitar shop we found was closed, and the unnaturally high quota of baseball caps and 'Everything's A Pound!' stores was spiritually unsettling – but something unfathomable dictated that we didn't quite feel ready to leave. As we'd watched Ed limp off up the street towards his snail-infested flat, cape flapping in the wind, we'd seen two teenage boys gesticulate and shout towards him from an adjacent street. The boys were roughly Peter's age, and their comments – not quite loud enough for Ed or us to hear, but loud enough to convince the teenagers, in their minuscule minds, that they were doing something extremely brave – almost certainly didn't relate to what a stylish fellow our busking friend was. It suddenly occurred to me that Ed might not have been wholly comfortable in Peter's presence. Teenagers were probably the bane of his existence. I wondered about Peter, and how he would have behaved towards Ed on his own, or with his friends.

'Were you unsettled by him?' I enquired, as we strolled along the seafront.

'Neh,' said Peter. 'Not really. I was a bit worried when he got the axe out. But that was sort of cool as well.'

'But his stories must have made you a bit sad?'

'Yeah, sort of. I dunno. But I thought he might have been making some stuff up. Like the women.' Ed had talked about 'girls' a lot – how their quality differed from town to town – in the manner that you might expect of someone a third of his age. 'He seemed to think he could pull anyone, which was weird, with him being so old and dressing like that. And the knife fights and that – I wasn't sure if they were true. And some of the bad stuff – he seemed to have, like, brought it upon himself. I mean, it was obvious he should have signed to that record label.'

'Yeah, but people were kind of naïve in the Sixties. They had lots of silly ideas about The Man, and sticking it to him. Ed was probably a bit like everyone else: he didn't want to sell his soul to the devil. But while everyone else just pretended, Ed actually followed the whole thing through. And look where it left him.'

'Yeah. Fighting Tapeworm.'

'You didn't fancy going to his flat then?'

'Neh.'

To me, Ed was properly three-dimensional: hyper-real. Half of me wanted to drive him back to London, offer him a bed for the night and put out his records for him. The other half was slightly frightened of him. For days, even weeks after I met him, he was there, at the edge of my conscience. I wanted to write a book about him, a film. Yet I already felt guilty for exploiting him by using him as part of Peter's education.

What I couldn't quite gauge was how real he was to Peter. How would he describe Ed to his friends? As a mad old guy who thought he was Robin Hood, or as a fascinating relic? Would he even mention him to them? When he got back to his natural environment, would he see Ed in the same way as the fourteen-year-old me had seen Daft George, the man who had minced up and down the lane where my gran lived, reciting poetry while dressed in a kaftan and a hard hat? In other words: in a small-minded way which ignored the baggage of personal history? It was hard to tell.

Back in the car, as we trundled along the coast road behind what seemed like every one of South East England's most wheezing, sluggish HGVs, Peter slipped into one of his stoical phases. That is to say, one of his even-more-stoic-than-normal phases. I liked to think he was chewing the morning's experience over, adding it to his psychological armour. On the other hand, I worried that I'd done the wrong thing, let him see too much too early in his apprenticeship. During the journey down to Hastings, I'd felt we'd been finally getting to know each other, talking almost constantly – about his karate classes, about rock stars, about soft drinks, about Goat Punishment – but now we were silent. Earlier, we'd alternated between the boxless tapes that resided permanently in my car (Styx, Aerosmith, The Pretty Things, Sly And The Family Stone) and the ones Peter had brought in his rucksack (Puddle Of Mudd, AC/DC, Slipknot), but now the radio seemed to have somehow tuned itself to Classic FM without either of us noticing. The silence, punctured only by Peter crunching his fourth bag of McCoys in as many hours, was something cinematic and profound – pregnant with the understanding that when something was finally said, it would have to sum things up in the deepest manner imaginable. Normally, I would have broken it, but my pedagogical instinct told me it would have to be Peter's job this time. So I waited patiently until, just as we approached Lewes, he finally turned around to speak, his face bustling with double-decker revelation.

'I've been thinking,' he said, 'about buying a new jacket.'

EDUCATING PETER

THE JACKET

'What's wrong with the one you're wearing?'

'It's not long enough.'

'Looks pretty long to me.'

'No. It's got to be longer. It's more goth for it to be longer. You should see Raf's – it's really long, like, soooo goth. A bit like the one Brandon Lee wears in *The Crow*.'

'Oh. *The Crow*. I remember that. Bit rubbish – all that brooding and silliness.'

'I love it.'

'It's a long time since I saw it.'

'He's just so awesome. And it's just so weird that he got killed while they were filming it.'

'Yeah – you wonder why on earth there would be real bullets in the gun, if it was just a movie set. Do you think that makes you like it more?'

'Mmmm. Dunno. Haven't really thought about it. Maybe.'

'I like Angel from *Buffy The Vampire Slayer* – he's

got a big billowy dark coat. I'm onto series five of that now, where Spike decides he loves Buffy. Dead good.'

'Uh.'

'So what else makes up the goth look, apart from the coat?'

'Well, big boots. And straight hair.'

'Yours is a bit curly, isn't it?'

'Yeah. It's really irritating. I try brushing it, but it just gets a sort of straw mushroom effect. It kind of looks better when it's wet.'

'I know what you mean. I had straight hair until I was fourteen, then I woke up one morning and it was like wire wool. Nothing I could do with it, and when I tried to grow it, it just went out, not down. It's kind of okay and straightish again now, but it only seemed to get okay when I stopped thinking about it.'

'I'm seriously thinking about getting mine straightened.'

'I'm not sure if I'd advise it. My cousin tried that and it started falling out, and the effect lasted virtually no time at all. She was well pissed off.'

'Really?'

'We sound a bit like girls, don't we?'

'A little bit.'

'I'm glad nobody can hear this conversation.'

'At least we don't run like girls.'

'Good point. Do you want to put some music on? This classical shit's alright in traffic jams but it's bugging the crap out of me now.'

'Okay. What?'

'What about that – the one on the floor, by your left

foot. Yeah, there, just under that Frazzles packet . . .
No, those are Wotsits.'

'Cheap Trick. Who are they?'

'People called them the metal Beatles. They're probably not heavy metal as you know it, but they do rock.
Don't worry – they don't use lutes. The guitarist has a
twelve-neck guitar or something . . . This song's ace;
it's what they used to start their concerts with. There's
another really good song a couple of tracks on that you
might know because Shakin' Stevens covered it.'

'Who's Shakin' Stevens?'

'Don't worry. Forget I said it.'

'Oh. I like this.'

CHEAP TRICK – *IN COLOR* (CBS, 1977)

Tom: 'Cheap Trick's second album is their best because its drums are like sofas for your ears, because Robin Zander's voice is the spirit of rock encapsulated, and because it features none of the sentimental goof boy indulgences or overproduction of the band's later work. It's a slicker record than the group's eponymous debut, but with just as much energy, and an example of guitars sounding as smooth as they should ever sound, but not a hair smoother. Here, the Trick, Chicago's finest, offer the perfect bridge between the best kind of hard rock chest-beating and new wave's burning immediacy. The record's sleeve, with the pretty boy half of the band pictured on the front, and the geek half pictured on the rear, sums up music which is just as playful and dangerous on the inside as it is sweet and shiny on the outside.

'If the songs on *In Color* were potential suitors for your daughter, they'd be somewhere between The Fonz and Matt Dillon, and would be certain to wink salaciously at you before they peeled out from the kerb outside your house. "I

Want You To Want Me", "Oh Caroline", "Downed", "Southern
Girls" – the majority of classic Trick is here, in its pouting,
yearning pomp. None of it lasts more than three minutes,
none of it leaves you less than dizzy, none of it takes the
blindest bit of notice that, somewhere to its east, punk is in
its heyday. Zander, Tom Petersson, Rick Nielsen and Bun E.
Carlos don't care about revolution; they care about motor-
bikes, skinny ties, your sixteen-year-old daughter and amp
specifications. They also leave you in no doubt that these
things are the essence of high-adrenalin music, and that
you'd be greedy to want anything more.'

Peter: 'I like this. It's a bit cheesy, but sort of cool, too.
The bit where the bloke groans in the middle eight on that
song "Southern Girls" – that's good. I just wish it would get
a bit heavier sometimes, y'know. They look a bit wankerish
on the cover. I mean, all that big hair and cowboy boots
stuff. Weeeeird. I dunno. They probably really regret it, now
they're so old. When was this made? 1967 or something.
That's probably before The Beatles, isn't it? It's probably
quite heavy for when it was made. I might have quite liked it
if I'd been young then. It's hard to say, really, y'know? I think
my dad would like it. You can tell they're dead good on
guitar, though – probably at least as good as Sam. Raf
would probably say they were boring fogies, though. I just
wish they'd shout a bit sometimes. But at least it rocks. Not
like some of that wimpy folk stuff we listened to on the way
down to Hastings. All that stuff about dragons and peddlers
and letting people steal your thyme. Not so sure about that,
really.'

EDUCATING
PETER

HERO PUNISHMENT

The unassumingly stylish, angular car – a Mustang? a Dodge? – rolled up the side of the valley and drew softly to a halt. Two men, their shirts blaring, their sideburns painstakingly cultivated, emerged. They'd left the bad guys a couple of canyons behind, eating their dust.

'Yep,' said Lightfoot. 'Transmission's gone. Cadillac's my car, anyway.'

'Where are we now?' said Thunderbolt.

'Hell's canyon. Snake river,' replied Lightfoot.

'You're better off getting as far away from me as you can, kid.'

'In for a penny, in for a pound.'

'Lonely country, kid. You got any folks?'

'You know what? I don't even know any more. That's weird.'

I turned the television off, retrieving my Windolene wipes from the top of the set.

You had to hand it to the road movies of the 1970s.

Some of them might not have aged as well as others, but the fact was that all of them were very good at making the experience of high adventure on the open highway seem real and exciting. When it came to recreating the dreaming, the drugs, the drink, the violence and the guttural engine noises, you couldn't really fault them. I could confirm this, of course, because I too was now an established road warrior, with at least a modicum of experience of all of these things (if you really think about it, Wheat Crunchies are a kind of drug, aren't they?). Yet I couldn't help feeling that some of my favourite directors had missed one major element – something that every road tripper has to deal with, sooner or later, no matter how long he avoids it; something which, in its own way, is as hair-raising as a race against the County Sheriff to the state line, as spine-chilling as having a phantom juggernaut bearing down on you from the wrong side of the road, and as intrinsic to the outlaw experience as being chased by a truckload of bloodthirsty rednecks.

Cleaning.

The puzzling thing was, when I'd been in the car with Peter I hadn't really got the impression he'd made that much mess. Sure, he'd munched his way through two family-size multi-packs of crisps, four Mars Bars, two Burger King value meals and a packet of sherbet lemons, but now, as I returned to the car and searched in vain for a vacuum cleaner attachment sophisticated enough to fit down the gap between the passenger seat and the ashtray, I found myself gazing at the carnage before me in something halfway between reverence and outrage. Where had that spearmint Polo wrapper come from? Who had hidden that half-eaten doughnut in the glove compartment? And why, when Thunderbolt and Lightfoot stopped in a valley, did you never see Clint Eastwood trying to prise a half-sucked mint imperial off the carpet beneath the clutch pedal, while Jeff Bridges stood poised behind him with his finger on the trigger of a bottle of Febreeze?

'I thought you were doing this journey with one teenager, not ten,' said my wife, Edie, who, clearly tired of overhearing me make noises like 'mmmrrr', 'jjjrrr' and 'ohmygodwhat'sthat?', had come out to see what all the fuss was about.

It was exactly twelve hours since the end of my first segment of adventures with Peter. We'd parted on good terms, promising to meet again in a fortnight's time – karate classes, fencing lessons, a visit to his dad's place and a couple of parties were going to make it impossible for him to see me again before then – and not to let on to Jenny about the snack food. I'd driven home, woken up wired from a dream about more driving, then spent the morning alternating between the Ford Focus in the driveway and the *Thunderbolt And Lightfoot* and *Vanishing Point* videos in the living room. I felt that, all in all, our quest was progressing successfully and fulfilling Jenny's criteria of 'ammunition' for Peter's decisions about his future. Something, though, was unsettling me, and I couldn't quite put a name to it. It wasn't the endless litter. It wasn't the boarded-up waxwork museum. It wasn't the sixty-pound parking ticket that I'd had slapped on my windscreen in Hastings after being distracted by

Ed The Troubadour and his tights. It wasn't even the fact that, towards the end of our journey back to Crouch End, when I'd put the first Grand Funk Railroad album in the tape player, Peter had sneakily slipped on his Walkman headphones. Instead, it was something to do with the way Thunderbolt stopped, gazed up at the big American sky and leaned on his car, as if it was a friend he'd be able to trust for ever in the grand game of survival. It was something to do with the monotony of the A11, particularly on the stretch between Barton Mills and Newmarket. It was something to do with the way people didn't signal when they were going right in filter lanes. It was something to do with the way the Ford Focus went 'brumm' and not 'raaaargh'. And yes, okay, it was just a tiny little bit to do with the litter.

To put it more bluntly, it was driving: I wasn't enjoying it as much as I should have been.

It's difficult to convey exactly how difficult it was to admit this to myself. Having taken and passed my driving test at the earliest possible opportunity, been in possession of a car for most of my adult life, and frequently enjoyed the bribing opportunities that go hand in hand with being The Kind Of Friend You Can Rely On For Lifts, I've always seen being a keen driver as a small yet important part of my self-image. That is to say, I have never thought of a car in sexual terms, don't know a carburettor from a graphic equaliser, do none of my own repairs, yet regularly drool over Aston Martins, once described fifth gear as 'creamy', and look down slightly on male friends without a licence in the way that you would on people who'd never had a girlfriend. I like cars. I like the way they make you feel like an adult, yet can fulfil your kid fantasies. I like the way that, if you think about it properly, they're just dodgems and go-karts on a bigger scale. I like the way they turn the world into a free-spirited place with beaches and fields and lakes, rather than a bunch of interconnected urban sprawls which just happen to have train stations and bus stations and airports.

In reverie form, I'd seen the process of educating Peter as being *about* cars. About music, yes, and about Peter's future, sure, but essentially, on an existential level, about cars. Driving fast in them. Gazing out of them wistfully. Using them to take you somewhere special. However, here I was, a fifth of the way into our journey – a journey which, if I was honest with myself, probably wasn't going to be quite as geographically diverse as I'd hoped, owing to Peter's chock-a-block school and social life – and I was feeling as though if I drove again in the next year, it would be a lifetime too soon. Somehow, in the world that Peter and I had inhabited for the last few days, the on-road experience wasn't quite the same as it was in *Thunderbolt And Lightfoot*. In fact, it wasn't an 'experience' at all; just a normal trip in a family car, which took you where you wanted to go in (if you were lucky) as little time as possible.

It wasn't as if I hadn't tried my best. On the way along the coast to Hastings, I'd pulled over on a grassy verge and stared out towards the English Channel, pondering the meaning of life, thinking that this was a road movie kind of thing to do, but Peter had looked at me strangely and opted to stay in the car, and I'd returned to the Ford Focus feeling a little bit sheepish and silly. Later, I'd thought about livening things up by ditching the Focus and hotwiring a nearby Vauxhall Vectra, but decided against it on the basis that, if I'd freaked out about getting a parking ticket, I was going to find it difficult affecting a devil-may-care attitude about driving a vehicle with 'hot' plates.

However, I was determined not to give up. After all, I was probably tired from racking up 500 miles and talking to a teenager non-stop for two days, and hence hadn't had the brain space to think about the matter creatively.

'There's a chance you're being a little too hard on yourself about this,' said Edie later that night.

'Hard in what way?' I said.

'Well, you're blaming yourself. Has it ever occurred to you that the reason you're not getting that authentic road trip ambience might be the car, and not you?'

'How do you mean?'

'It's just . . . it's a Ford Focus.'

'Yeah – it's comfortable, reliable, does quite a high rate of miles to the gallon, and it's got one of those stereos that gets louder in perfect step with your revs. What's wrong with it? I weighed up the options and decided it was the best car for the trip.'

'I thought you bought it so we could fit big furniture in the back, and because that cricket bloke took the piss out of your Fiesta.'

'Well, yeah. But for the trip as well.'

'It's just, well, you can't really imagine Steve McQueen driving it, can you?'

'He might. I mean, he drove one of those Ford Puma things for that advert.'

'But that was computer-generated.'

'Oh yeah.'

'All I'm saying is that, well, you might want something that makes you feel a bit . . . sexier.'

In the three years that I've known her, a couple of recurring themes have emerged in conversations between my wife and me. One of them is my vulnerability and unworldliness. The other is her all-reaching wisdom about the world and everything in it. I'd learned to trust her judgement, and not simply on matters of a gentle and womanly nature. Hence, several days later, I found myself in the reception area of one of Norfolk's premier vehicle hire establishments, talking height specifications with a rangy man with a limp and a bright red jacket with a name badge pinned to it that said 'Clive – Assistant Haulage Executive'.

A van! Of course! The answer to all my problems! The only thing I couldn't work out was why I hadn't had the ounce of brain cells required to think of it before. The list of points in its favour was almost as long as Thunderbolt's sideburns:

1. It was the traditional mode of transport for thousands of struggling rock groups.
2. It would make me feel like a big man.
3. It would be a less banal mode of transport for Peter, thus making him respect me as a hip, impulsive dude, rather than someone slightly younger and less boring than his parents.

4. If we happened to run into a famous band who wanted to be our friends and needed a lift somewhere, we'd have no trouble fitting their equipment in the back.

5. Its gear-stick would probably be up near the dashboard, which was really cool.

6. It would stop men with fat necks in BMWs bullying me at roundabouts.

7. It would allow me to bully men with fat necks in BMWs at roundabouts.

8. If I was lucky, it might get dusty, and someone with a sense of humour might write 'Clean me!' or 'Shaz blows buffalo' on its back door with their finger.

9. It was just the kind of crazy, nonsensical idea that I'd envisaged my adventure with Peter being all about.

10. I didn't have to keep it if I decided it was crap.

Full of renewed vigour, I followed Clive The Assistant Haulage Executive into a small room with a glass coffee table and a picture of Lady Diana on the wall. He reached for a ring binder from the shelf behind him.

'So you're saying you want a Luton?'

'I'm not sure,' I said. 'I think so. At least, if that's what we had before from you, when we moved house last year.'

'Well, did it look like this?' Clive The Assistant Haulage Executive held up a picture of a quite big white van. It looked like a lot of other quite big white vans.

'I think so, but I'm not certain. It could have been bigger. Or perhaps smaller.'

'Well, can you remember if it had a tail-lift?'

What was a tail-lift? 'Yeah. Actually, I think it did.'

'Okay. We're getting somewhere. What kind of stuff are you shifting? Is it another house move?'

'No. Not really.'

'Well, is there a lot of heavy or long equipment – settees, beds, shelves?'

'Not really.'

'Well what kind of stuff are you moving?'

'The thing is, you see, I'm sort of not moving anything.'

'Nothing at all?'

'Nothing.'

'Well, why do you need it?'

'I just want to drive a van.'

'Oh. In that case I suppose you can take your pick.'

I looked out of the window to a row of transits. They didn't look quite as much like the A-Team's van as I'd hoped, but that didn't seem to matter now. You remember this? I thought to myself, as I drew Clive's attention towards a vehicle that looked slightly less muddy and worn-out than its contemporaries. This is what freedom feels like.

It had been an eventful fortnight for Peter, in my absence. First, he'd gone up a belt in karate, then, at a friend's party the same night, he'd kissed the daughter of a minor TV chef. It had been a heat-of-the-moment thing, a direct product of his elation at the new belt, but now the girl was following him around, sending him notes during Geography and saying he looked like the guitarist in Staind, a new metal band that Peter didn't even like.

Somewhere in the midst of all this, Toast Hero, the band that he looked upon as his lo-fidelity side project, had split up. Except they weren't called Toast Hero any more; they were called Toast Punishment. Goat Punishment, meanwhile – who, I was relieved to hear, were still going strong – were now called Goat Hero. The name switch had been suggested by Peter's friend Raf, who'd decided that Goat Hero suited the nature of his new songs better, and subsequently approved by the three members of Toast Hero (two of whom were also members of Goat Punishment anyway). But now, with Toast Punishment no more, all of this seemed something of a moot point.

'I mean, technically,' I suggested to Peter, 'now Toast Punishment have gone, Goat Hero could be called Goat Hero or Toast Punishment without anyone having any problem with it.'

Toast Punishment had disintegrated because Sam, the guitarist, had grouped together with Tiger, the drummer, and put forward a motion to introduce rapping and sampling into the group's sound. Peter, who hated all rap music, had recoiled in terror at this suggestion and threatened to leave, then gone around to Raf's house and told Raf about his growing dissatisfaction with Sam's insistence on inserting words like 'yo', 'homey' and 'beeaaatch' into his lyrics. This had somehow got back to Sam, and the group had imploded in the school's quadrangle at breaktime. Peter knew that Raf, who'd long been pressing for him to leave his side project, had probably been stirring things up, but he didn't care. Toast Punishment, he told me philosophically, were only meant to be great for a short time, and that time had passed.

'Did you ever get around to recording a demo?' I asked.

'Not in the end, no,' said Peter.

I was glad that Peter now felt able to share the more intricate details of his life with me, and I wondered if in some small way it was my fresh means of transport that was inspiring the new confidence. I'd decided to leave the van as a surprise until I arrived to pick him up, and his reaction had been encouraging, pitched somewhere between disbelief and confusion. Now, as we approached Waterloo Bridge in the tail-end of London's all-day rush hour, he seemed less slumped in his seat than usual. Edie had joined us for the trip, and Peter appeared far less withdrawn in her presence than he'd been during his first day in mine. Moreover, despite the fact that we'd been listening to the *The Best Of Steely Dan* for the last fifty minutes, he'd managed to refrain from putting his Walkman on.

On the opposite bank of the Thames, about half a mile away, we could just make out the lights of the Royal Festival Hall, where, in half an hour or so, we would meet up with my friends Steve and Sue, and take our seats to watch a rare performance by one of my favourite songwriters of all time: Brian Wilson from The Beach Boys. It would be the first gig that Peter and I had attended together, but I wasn't certain he knew what was in store for him.

'What kind of place is the Royal Festival Hall?' he'd asked me earlier.

'Oh, it's a big place. Very posh. All-seated. Expensive drinks,' I'd replied.

'Seated? So there won't be any moshing, then?'

'Er, I doubt it. People might sway from side to side quite vigorously, though.'

Peter, it transpired, knew three Beach Boys songs: 'the one with the weird video that they always show on VH-1', 'the one about surfing' and 'the one about California'. He thought his dad had a copy of their *Pet Sounds* album, but wasn't quite sure, and was fairly certain he'd never been exposed to its delights. There was, of course, no reason that he should have been, yet I couldn't help inwardly gasping on hearing this. There were a few occasions during my time with Peter when it suddenly, fully dawned on me just how young he was, and this was one of them. Wasn't it weird, I found myself musing, that people were still being born as late as 1988? Somehow, the idea seemed deeply wrong, a cruel trick played by some malevolent god: the only hit single The Beach Boys had scored during Peter's lifetime was their risible 1989 nostalgia-fest, 'Kokomo'.

It was hard enough to explain the legend of The Beach Boys to someone who *did* think *Pet Sounds* was their greatest album, let alone someone who'd never heard it and was under the impression that the group only recorded one song about surfing. Between trying to manoeuvre the transit around irate taxis and sense-less bus drivers, I attempted to fill Peter in on the essential elements of the group's story: the early good-time hits followed by the descent into madness and darkness, friendship with Charles Manson and strange songs about worms. To me, this was stuff that had been repeated by so many deferential rock critics that even grazing the subject seemed like a monumental cliché. But to Peter it was new and mysterious. Or – as was equally likely – plain boring and fogeyish.

The career of Brian Wilson, who'd written the vast majority of The Beach Boys' best songs, was currently enjoying an Indian summer of sorts, which was a good job, since its ordinary summer had been unnaturally curtailed. During the late Sixties, I explained to Peter, Wilson had gone into hiding, taking vast amounts of acid, writing the odd classic orchestral pop song and leaving the rest of the band to tour without him. Wilson was pop's saddest casualty, and endless stories circulated about his strange domestic habits. He insisted, so the legend went, on having his feet in a sandbox as he composed on the piano, and when fellow icons like Paul McCartney and Phil Spector came to his house to wish him well, he locked himself in his garden shed and hid from them, convinced they were there to harm him. Yet, with just Wilson's rare bursts of inspiration and stockpiled demos to draw from, the remaining Beach Boys continued to make terrific records, with Wilson's younger brothers, Carl and Dennis, finding a strength in their own song-writing abilities that frequently surpassed their older brother's. These – 1970's *Sunflower*, 1971's *Surf's Up*, 1972's *Carl And The Passions* and 1973's *Holland* – were shadowier, more damaged albums than before, but, in the eyes of many, even more beautiful than their more famous mid-Sixties predecessors.

The oldest Wilson spent most of the Seventies in bed, apparently rehearsing for a Grizzly Adams look-alike contest. His weight ballooned, then the fat seemed to fall off him overnight, but in neither state did he look healthy. The late Seventies and early Eighties saw him make a series of aborted comeback attempts, but his mental state remained fragile, and wasn't aided by the efforts of a psychiatrist, who, it was said at the time, turned him into a nervous wreck who had to ask permission before going to the toilet. Carl and Dennis, meanwhile, hung out with Ronald Reagan, fell off yachts to a watery death and recorded 'Kokomo'. But now the psychiatrist had been seen off by Wilson's family and friends, and Wilson was finally back on the road, singing songs he'd never sung live before, with a backing band he considered better than The Beach Boys in their prime.

Over the last couple of years, I'd become friends with this band, meeting up for bangers and mash with them when they were in the UK. They were called The Wondermints and, when they weren't working with Wilson, they made great records of their own, bursting with sunshine melodies and a rhapsody of impenetrable lyrics about outer-space and underwater love. The leading figures in the group were Darian and Nick, both of whom were chiefly recognisable by the unusual outline of their heads. Nick was never seen without a furry Russian hat, while Darian had a quiff of such immense size and wiriness that it wasn't unheard of for complete strangers to request to touch it in public. Each was an unimpeachably nice guy obsessed with good food and antique keyboards. It was Nick and Darian who'd been responsible for obtaining tickets for us for tonight, a show which had sold out within hours of being advertised.

'Uh. Mmmff,' said Peter, when I'd finished relating this to him. The tone of the 'mmmff' seemed to hint towards at least a buried modicum of awe for the story, but without Jenny's superior translation skills it was difficult to tell for sure.

I'd wanted to take Peter not just to a gig, but to an event, and this, quite clearly, was what this evening was set to be. To our immediate rear sat Bobby Gillespie, frontman for the dance-rockers turned electro-nihilists Primal Scream – a proper rock star whose hard-living, tough-talking rebel credentials were denigrated only by his rumoured passion for organic vegetables. To our left sat Ray Davies, former leader of The Kinks. To our right sat Colin Larkin, a man who was rumoured to have the largest record collection in Britain. It was clear that Wilson, who'd once been the brittle genius behind America's biggest band, was now a cult hero on an unprecedented scale. Would he be fat, thin? Would he have a sandbox with him? Would he sing 'Surf's Up'? The low humming sound in the air was that of a few thousand people wondering these things. Just one voice seemed defiantly out of tune.

'Everyone's so old,' whispered Peter, surreptitiously munching his way through a bag of Frazzles.

'I don't know. What about him?' I pointed to a lanky, bleach-haired kid of about seventeen, taking his seat a couple of rows ahead of us.

'Mmm. Suppose.'

'Don't worry. Just think: you'll be a step ahead of all your friends after this. In a few years, everyone will think you're really cool for liking The Beach Boys.'

'You reckon?'

'I promise. I used to think Beach Boys stuff was old and boring when I was your age, too.'

'It's not that I think it's old and boring. Just, y'know, not very heavy.'

'But don't you think it would be a good move for Goat Hero to be influenced by something not very heavy? That could be really subversive.'

'Neh. That would just be silly.'

Thus far in his life, Peter had been to see five live bands: Offspring, Kitty, Slipknot, Linkin Park and AC/DC. It wasn't a vast amount of experience, but even if it had been, I felt sure that the next two hours would give him a glimpse of a different kind of hero worship – nothing to do with showmanship, or shock value, or heaviness, or risk.

Wilson, it turned out, was neither fat nor slim, but somewhere in between. Each time he arrived on stage – for the normal set, and for the trio of encores that followed – he jogged to his seat in the manner of a slightly absurd uncle miming out everyday actions for his three-year-old nephew. During each song, he acted out lyrics – a small circle with his hands for 'sun', a hand on his heart for 'love', a finger pointed towards the audience for 'you' – and, as each came to a close, he turned to the audience and asked, 'Wasn't that a lovely little song?' The whole routine had a way of turning grown men into milksops, and seemed to be having the same effect on the nihilists behind us as repeated viewings of *Steel Magnolias* tended to have on broody housewives. Everywhere you looked, people seemed to be striving to win a Who Loves Brian

The Most? contest. Yet Brian wasn't stylish, or hand-some, and he certainly didn't rock. He was just a slightly simple-looking guy with a goofy smile and an emotionally naked way with a melody. If you were an alien, sent to the Royal Festival Hall to study the habits of human life forms, you'd find the scene quite hard to grasp. If you were a melancholy teenager, you might find it even harder. I wasn't completely sure *I* understood it.

After the show, Darian supplied the five of us with tickets for the aftershow party. I liked to think that this was because I'd complimented him on his quiff the last time I'd seen him, but I knew that it was more likely to be a gesture aimed in the direction of Steve and Sue.

Among those closest to them, Steve and Sue were known as The Goldens, both because of the colour of their hair and the shining inspiration of their person-alities. In modern music industry terms they were a genuine phenomenon of fandom: a couple of people who had no financial ties to the music industry, could offer a musician nothing in terms of sexual or career-orientated gain, yet were fast friends with a huge number of bands. If you were a musician making Sixties-style pop in America, slightly eccentric, and had had a record out in the late Nineties or early Noughties, the chances are you would have exchanged a compilation tape with them. Their home was a con-stant thoroughfare of psychedelic drifters, wayfaring strummers and rag-tag power-poppers, to the extent that extra room for their guests (and Darian's quiff) had been a major factor in their last house move. Most weirdly of all, they did it all for love.

In short, they were good people for Peter to be around.

Although it was already ten thirty, and I'd promised Jenny that Peter would be home not much later than eleven, I felt the chance to go backstage was too important a part of his training to pass up. Also, it was obvious this would be no normal celebrity party filled with the usual music industry liggers and poseurs. Tonight, explained Darian, there would be two parties: the one upstairs, which people pretended was the party, and the one downstairs, where the real action was. I thought the concept seemed somewhat dishonest, and said a lot about the corrupt nature of the music business.

'So which one are our passes for?' I asked him.

'Oh, the *real* one,' said Darian.

'Great!' I said, punching the air.

Down and down The Wondermints led us, through the bowels of the Festival Hall, until it seemed we could only drop out of its bottom onto something hard. Eventually we found ourselves in a lift the size of a small car, already stuffed full of eager-looking Americans complimenting one another on their knowledge of obscure Farfisa keyboards. Peter looked scared, his mouth tight, his eyes jerking to our right. I followed them to the corner of the lift, where a bulky-ish, square-jawed man of around sixty stood humming to himself. He looked kind of familiar.

Very familiar.

Darian had already talked about the possibility of 'meeting Brian', and I'd had mixed feelings about the issue. On the one hand, he was Brian Wilson. On the other hand, you had to take into account The Jonathan Richman Factor. The Jonathan Richman Factor was my term for the fundamental disappointment that goes with meeting your musical heroes. I call it The Jonathan Richman Factor in memory of the time that I'd met Jonathan Richman, the acoustic punk mooncalf, and, instead of wanting to talk about all the songs he'd written that I loved, he'd wanted to talk about his fascination with the construction trade. Wilson wasn't close to my heart in quite the way that Richman was – I'd discovered The Beach Boys too late in life – but he was still slightly unreal to me, and I wasn't sure I wanted him to be anything more tangible.

Now I was stuck in a lift with him, and it was decision time. As the lift descended, Sue, Steve, Peter, Edie and I silently began to psych each other out with a series of starey eye and twitchy mouth movements. Even without sounds, the dialogue taking place here – a series of 'That's . . . ?', 'I *know*', 'Well . . . go on then' and 'No, why don't you, if you're so brave?', and 'Piss off, coward' type comments – was obvious to all involved. Everyone knew that the one who made the first move would be held fully responsible for his or her actions. No-one seemed quite able to take that step.

After what seemed like at least three eternities, the lift rumbled to a halt, ejecting our hero into a bright white corridor. Peter was the first to speak, confusion painted all over his face.

'Why didn't you talk to him? I thought you thought he was brilliant.'

'I'm not sure I would have known what to say,' I said.

'You could have at least told him you enjoyed the show,' said Peter.

'But what if that was all I got to say to him – "great show"? I'm not sure I could have lived with that.'

'Uh,' said Peter. 'Yeah.'

We found ourselves in a dimly lit, orangey underground bar. Brian had disappeared – possibly to brush up on his pretend jogging – but several of his most eminent spiritual apprentices were keeping the barman busy in his absence. It seemed everyone in the UK who was in a band who sounded even the tiniest bit like The Beach Boys was in this room, along with at least half of their American contemporaries. Picking up a Coke for Peter and beers for the rest of us, I joined the others in an inconspicuous corner and began the surveillance process.

This, generally, was what I did at aftershow parties, on the few occasions I still went to them: I watched. Every now and again, I would get involved in a lengthy and embarrassingly anally retentive conversation about early Tom Petty And The Heartbreakers albums with a guitarist from an American power-pop band. But on the whole I took a silent, back-seat role in proceedings. Tonight was no different, apart from the fact that with Peter there I felt slightly more self-conscious about it. He seemed unusually quiet, and I couldn't tell whether this was because he was bored, intimidated, tired, or just waiting for me to do something interesting. I put myself in his shoes and decided that if I was fourteen, I, too, might have expected something slightly more exciting to happen at a backstage party.

'That's thingy, isn't it?' he said, nodding towards a helmet-haired man surrounded by women in leather jackets.

'I think so, yeah,' I said.

'And isn't that that guy?' he said.

'What? Him? Yeah. Looks a bit smaller in real life, doesn't he?' I said.

It was heartening to know that Peter was familiar with some of the celebrities here. Shortly after we'd arrived, I'd had a five-minute conversation with Ray Davies from The Kinks – five minutes, because of all the Americans wanting to come up and tell him just how much 'Waterloo Sunset' had enhanced their life – whom I'd interviewed for a music magazine a couple of years ago. Davies had been friendly and, to my immense surprise, actually remembered me, and I'd hoped Peter might be impressed – even if you hadn't heard of Davies, his thick mane of hair and proud posture would have told you he was someone important – but when I'd returned to my seat he'd merely smiled vaguely and shrugged. But now Peter had his eyes on Richard Ashcroft, the former lead singer of The Verve.

'I can't believe he's here!' said Peter.

'Why not?' I said.

'Well, he's . . . Some of *my* mates like his music.'

'Well, yeah. There are a lot of young people who like The Beach Boys, you know. But I'm not going to go and speak to him, if that's what you're thinking.'

'I wasn't.'

The party was breaking up, and Ashcroft, shielded by a forcefield of cagoule-wearing men with Seventies footballer haircuts slightly less expensive than his own, was leaving. You knew he was leaving because he was obviously the kind of person who wouldn't have been able to leave a room inconspicuously if he'd tried. He probably couldn't clean his teeth without swaggering slightly in the process. We watched as he and his reserve haircuts strutted their way towards the swing door at the end of the corridor. There was a pause. Then we watched again as, realising that they had entered the kitchen, they turned around and made their way back. Then, finally, we watched some more as they called the lift and tried manfully to adopt an aura of insouciance while waiting for it to creak down to the right floor.

Shortly afterwards, we, too, made our way to the exit. The five of us had our differing views on Brian Wilson and the exact degree of his genius, but we were all agreed on one point: the night had reached its peak.

EDUCATING PETER

SALLY

'So you enjoyed it then?'

'I wouldn't say "enjoyed". It was . . . interesting.'

' "Interesting"? That's normally what people say as a put-down, isn't it?'

'No, no, it was cool. It was just, I thought they could have made more of their guitars. I mean that guy – the one with the silly hat – he was using a Danelectro Twelve. You can get really cool sustain with those. Or maybe it was a Fender Jazzmaster.'

'Oh. Can't say I noticed. But you liked the songs, yeah? The harmonies and stuff?'

'I suppose. Mmmm. Er. Yeah. They were pretty nice.'

'And what about the backstage party?'

'Mmm. It was good. I thought there would be more . . . going on.'

'What do you think you'll tell your mates about it?'

'I'll tell them about Richard Ashcroft, definitely.'

'You'd have to really, wouldn't you? It kind of

reminded me of *Spinal Tap* – y'know, what happened with the lift.'

'*Spinal Tap*? I think I've heard of it. I'm not sure.'

'Oh, wow, you've never seen *Spinal Tap*? You *have* to see *Spinal Tap*. I'll lend it to you. It's the funniest film ever. It's all about this heavy metal band who go on tour in America but I won't go on any more because I'll just end up talking about it for hours and reciting loads of catchphrases that you've never heard of. But the thing is, that thing with Ashcroft, it really reminded me of a scene in the film where the band get lost backstage and can't find their way to the stage.'

'Uh. Sounds cool.'

'So what's next for Goat Hero?'

'I dunno. We're rehearsing next Wednesday.'

'I'd love to hear some stuff.'

'I'm not sure you'd like it.'

'I might. I like some of the stuff you like. We both like AC/DC.'

'Yeah. But not many of my friends like AC/DC.'

'What about the girl whose dad's a TV chef? Whatshername? Does she like them?'

'Sally? Don't talk about her. She thought, like, Darius was cool until about two and a half minutes ago, when she suddenly decided to like nu-metal.'

'Is that because of you?'

'I dunno. Don't care.'

'Why? Is she not attractive?'

'She's just kind of immature. There was this girl she used to hang around with, Hannah? And they just used to go round poking people in the ribs at break-time. I mean, she was in year eight at the time.'

'Year eight? So what's that in old-fashioned terms. Second year? Used to—'

'Not sure.'

'—be different when I was at school.'

'Oh, right.'

'So – poking people? What was that all about? Was that a flirting thing?'

'No. I dunno. It was just, like, really sad. Just poking people! They used to wear their hair in pigtails, too.'

'Not very goth?'

'Neh.'

'And now she likes Staind?'

'Says she does, yeah. And anyway, they're just sooo not the best nu-metal band. Raf and me hate them. They're kind of seriously fake.'

'So there are different degrees of quality in nu-metal? I never realised that. I thought all those bands sounded phoney and corporate.'

'No. No way.'

'Oh, right.'

'What's psychedelia?'

'Why?'

'I just wondered. What's the definition of it? 'Cos you're always going on about it. And all your mates and everyone seemed to be talking about it tonight.'

VARIOUS ARTISTS – NUGGETS: ORIGINAL ARTYFACTS FROM THE FIRST PSYCHEDELIC ERA (RHINO BOX SET, 1999)

Tom: 'In modern rock music, six years represents an evolutionary microsecond: enough time for Elastica, My Bloody Valentine and The Stereo MCs to record an album (if they all formed one supergroup, put in overtime and cut down on fag breaks). But by 1972, 1966 – the bloom year of America's garage punk movement – was a period rendered indistinct by at least a couple of aeons' worth of musical revolutions. If you even remembered it, you were a card-carrying historian.

'Lenny Kaye, a rock critic who moonlighted as a guitarist for Patti Smith, was such a historian. Disenchanted with rock's tendency for pomposity in the early Seventies, Kaye masterminded the original *Nuggets* album from his own singles collection – picking twenty-seven low-budget fleeting classics recorded in the suburban garages and cheapo recording studios of America between 1965 and 1968. Was he aware that he was sewing the seeds of punk? Doubtful. But trace a line back from the King's Road in 1977, via the

East Village in 1974, and you'll end up here, cradling the genre's raw, overenthusiastic genesis.

'By 1972, most of *Nuggets'* DIY John Townshends and Pete Lennons had long since swallowed their dreams of stardom for jobs at post offices and insurance companies; only the odd few grew into internationally famous pop innovators (Nazz's Todd Rundgren) and squirrel-shooting metal maniacs (The Amboy Dukes' Ted Nugent). On *Nuggets*, though, they sound like two-bit crooks who'd kidnap your mother, joyride her around the neighbourhood, and give her the best time she'd ever had.

'Kaye secured their place in the Sixties canon and recognised that they weren't just derivative trash, but some of the greatest singles bands in history. Most of them had only one single in them, but it was invariably more than the sum of its parts, a scuzz-caked, phlegm-baked blast of attitude over aptitude concocted on the cheapest out-of-tune guitar in Pisswolf, Idaho, or Candlelicker, Illinois. *Nuggets* – justifiably extended on this box set to a 118-track marathon – is one of those rare albums that seems on the verge of bursting into flames from beginning to end. Those volts of excitement you can hear are the waves of electricity that the British invasion left behind: the mind-altering radiation that escaped when a million American teenagers heard the thrilling, squalid central riff of The Kinks' "You Really Got Me". Some Nuggeteers made carbon copies of their heroes' music (play the Knickerbockers' "Lies" to a Beatlemaniac and watch them squirm), but most simply didn't have the talent or the patience. Through their boundless gusto and frantic inelegance, they made another form of equally cool, world-changing music by accident. Ever wondered what The Doors would have sounded like if they'd been sneering small-time hooligans without girlfriends? Check out The Seeds' "Pushin' Too Hard".

'Groups like The Standells and The Sonics were inhabiting a pretend macho world where they looked like Mick Jagger, played guitar like Jimmy Page and were the bedtime fantasy of every girl on their street. When you were a dis-enfranchised, possibly virgin, male bursting with testosterone, it must have been a great place to live. To hear Minneapolians The Litter howling "Hey Miss High And Mighty/Walking Right Awn By Me/That's Your Last Mistake" then attempting to make a two-dollar guitar sound like a sitar through a broken amplifier on "Action Woman" is to hear the essence of *Nuggets*: pseudo-sexual prowess plus playground sexism plus angst plus pseudo-satanic howling plus souped-up minimalist brilliance. *Nuggets* is the story of the psychedelic movement from the perspective of the people who couldn't afford drugs, replacing LSD with snot, fuzz and bile. It's the tale of the freaks and the outcasts who took over the garages and high school dances of Middle America. The sound of teenagers doing the exact thing they were invented for, doing it quickly, and doing it well.'

Peter: 'I can't believe a lot of these bands are teenagers. They sound so old, but maybe that's just 'cos the music's old. I like some of it. There's one song with a kind of duh, duh, duh, duh rhythm that's from that old film with those guys at the college with the togas. You know: the one with all the food fights and stuff. I don't know what the lyrics say – it sounds like the bloke's got false teeth, so it's hard to tell. All these bands sound like they've got something stuck in their mouth. But, yeah, that's a good song. And then there's another one, something about going to the centre of your mind, which has some nice FX on it – almost metal in a way. But a lot of it reminds me of people dancing in that way they do in *Austin Powers* films, with their arms flapping. It's probably kind of okay in a film and stuff, but I'm not sure I'd listen to it, like, at home. It's a bit buzzy-sounding, and I don't really . . . relate to it. At least I know what psychedelia is now. I thought this was it, but I wasn't sure. I thought there'd be more lyrics about heroin and stuff.'

EDUCATING PETER

HOMEWORK

When I was at secondary school, during the late Eighties, I had a friend called Richard Bush, who would play a game with his older sister called Pass The Cake. Fairly self-explanatory, the game involved the ongoing distribution of a dog-eared slice of chocolate cake, baked by Richard's mum in August 1988, between the two siblings' bedrooms. Neither would take responsibility for the cake, and both would rather set fire to their own limbs than admit defeat and take it downstairs. However, what started as a point of pride became something altogether weightier, reminiscent in its strategic planning of the most complex and clandestine war manoeuvre. As the months went by and it decomposed, the cake was secreted in more and more outlandish places – a shoe, a Trivial Pursuit box – often with a long-neglected toy soldier or Lego fireman protruding from it. Once, at the beginning of a Geography lesson, Richard found the cake waiting for him in his pencil case, decked out with rubbers for eyes, a Sellotape mouth and a pencil sharpener nose. Yet he refused to back down, despite the fact that by now, after all its manhandling, the cake had been reduced to a quarter of its original size. The following day, it was back in his sister's room, squashed between the pages of the latest issue of *Look-In* magazine.

'Who's on cake duty this morning?' was always the first thing I would say to Richard, when I called for him before school. Richard was a late riser, and it was my job to make sure he got up in time for our five past nine form meeting. This would normally involve me knocking at the door a dozen times, then amusing myself with Richard's sheepdog, Bracken, while Richard – one of the first kids in our school year to get stubble – shaved expansively, put a Move record on and thought up a new, ingenious place to hide the cake. On and off, I considered Richard my best friend, but I never quite sensed that the sentiment was reciprocated. Richard seemed above a concept like 'best friends' and, while popular at school, was generally considered an enigma: an astute classroom commentator whose sophisticated, mordant wit and taste in 'weird music from the old days' contradicted his callow years and made him, at heart, something of a loner. Still, it remains one of my bigger regrets in life that we lost touch, especially since now I listen to the exact same 'weird music from the old days' that our friends mocked him for listening to as a schoolboy. The last time I'd seen him had been in 1992, a year or so after leaving school, during a repugnantly worthy 'political scuzz-rock' fad in my musical development.

By that time, the cake survived merely as a hardened blue-ish crumb, the rest of it having been devoured by Bracken.

The more time I spent with Peter, the more I thought of Richard – partly because Peter, in his frequent bursts of age-belying perspicacity, often reminded me of him, but also because Peter and I were involved in our own ongoing version of Pass The Cake. In its lines of attack and resourcefulness, our adaptation of the game lived up to the one played by Richard and his sister in every way. There was only one difference: it wasn't a cake we were passing; it was a Blue Oyster Cult CD. Specifically, the one I'd advised Peter to buy in the Music And Video Exchange in Soho.

Somehow, the CD kept finding its way back into my possession. First, upon returning from Hastings, I'd found it stuffed beneath the back seat of the Ford Focus. I had to admit it seemed in some way significant that Peter had left this particular CD behind, rather than the nu-metal albums he'd purchased alongside it, but I'd given him the benefit of the doubt and politely returned it to him. But then, in the aftermath of Brian Wilson, I'd found it abandoned mysteriously in the glove compartment of the transit van. So now, recalling the rules of Pass The Cake, I'd decided to play dirty. As I sat in Peter's kitchen, watching Jenny (who'd been remarkably forgiving about our eighty-minute late arrival last night) pack Peter's lunchbox in the prelude to our next adventure together, I began to develop a plan. Today, I would suggest that we ate at Burger King, knowing that Peter would be powerless to resist. From there, implementing the different components of my killer strategy would be easy. It would be unfair to Jenny, and I'd feel guilty, but it would be worth it, and I had to suppress a sly little smile as I thought of tomorrow, when Peter would arrive home, unload his rucksack, open his lunchbox to throw away his uneaten organic lunch, and find one of the classic rock albums of 1976 positioned neatly between two slabs of wholemeal bread.

The day involved an early start for all of us. Edie and I were creaky and slow-witted from a night sleeping on the futon in Jenny's living room (although not slow-witted enough for me not to quickly switch the *Agents Of Fortune* CD with some Parma ham while Peter cleaned his teeth). Peter, meanwhile, was acting sheepishly. For lengthy periods of last night, at the Royal Festival Hall, it had slipped my mind that he was anything less than an adult, but this morning he was a fourteen-year-old again, being brashly instructed by his mother to take a bath, wrap up warm and re-member to eat his cucumber with hummus dip.

We were on our way, in a convoluted fashion, to Cambridge, to hunt for the reclusive former Pink Floyd singer Syd Barrett in the second leg of what I was thinking of as the Mavericks section of Peter's training (in other words: very much like the Loose Cannons section, but with a different name). First, we'd make the two-hour drive to my house, dropping Edie off and fetching for Peter what I was referring to as his first 'homework pack': a selection of background material that I thought would aid him in his musical studies. Then we'd head back down the A11 to one of my favourite British cities and go cult hero-hunting, with a stop for fast food along the way. All in all, I had a positive feeling about what the day held in store.

I'd had the idea about 'homework packs' the previous afternoon. It was no good, I'd decided, simply taking Peter out on trips, then returning him home and letting his capricious teenage mind forget about them. If I was going to give him something even remotely approaching a proper musical education, I had to get him thinking on my wavelength. He needed to be utterly consumed by our adventures; he also needed to be prepared, and in order to do that he needed homework and background revision. Rock and pop were, after all, scholarly subjects these days. Their finest achievements had aged too well to be written off as ephemeral trash.

Each time I met up with Peter, I decided, I would provide him with 'texts' which he would be expected to report back on. Would they all be actual texts? No – some of them would be records, some would be books, some would be films or documentaries – but I would call them all 'texts' anyway because it made me feel learned and important. I couldn't expect Peter to understand the natural gifts of Brian Wilson, coming in cold, having never listened to *Pet Sounds* or *Holland* – just as he couldn't expect me to understand *The Crow*, having never worn an enormous black jacket. From now on, he would be adequately prepared for our trips. His homework packs, though, wouldn't be limited to material that was relevant to our adventures; I would provide him with an entire didactic spectrum of rock and roll experience from the last four decades – good and bad, bizarre and straightforward. A 'text' could be a brilliant film, like *This Is Spinal Tap*, or it could be a rotten one, like *Sweetwater: A True Rock Story*. It could be a great album, like Big Star's *Radio City*, or it could be one composed entirely of what I deemed to be drab, scum-sucking brainrot, like The Stereophonics' *Performance And Cocktails*. It could be an eye-opening book of tales from Rock Babylon, like Nick Kent's *The Dark Stuff*, or it could be an impenetrable one of rambling egghead essays, like Greil Marcus's *Lipstick Traces*. It didn't matter – it would all help. More importantly, it would make me feel like I was a proper academic, and not just someone spending the best part of a year hanging around listening to music with a fourteen-year-old goth.

Two of Peter's first 'texts' were the cassettes I'd made for him of *The Madcap Laughs* and *Barrett*, the two undernourished solo albums that Syd Barrett had recorded during the early Seventies, following his exodus from Pink Floyd. My intention had been for Peter to take these home and spend some serious time pontificating over them, but since we were on our way to follow Barrett's trail, and they were the sort of albums you didn't want to be alone in a room with, I'd decided to play them in the van.

'Did they not have proper studios in those days, then?' said Peter, as the opening track of *The Madcap Laughs* wobbled into earshot.

Earlier, the transit had developed a fresh rattle in the region of the undercarriage directly beneath my left foot. Now it was impossible to distinguish rattle from lo-fi sonic experiment. I glanced across at Peter. The look on his face seemed to reflect all my uncertainty about what I was putting him through. Did he think I liked this music? I hoped not. Being careful not to steer the van into a fat-necked man's BMW, but not too careful, I strained to find the melody of the song over the grunt of the diesel engine, feeling certain it had involved a guitar at some point. It was the sort of album that gave you an involuntary squint.

I'd often wondered, during my time writing about rock music, if there was a mandatory contract that someone had forgotten to give me at the beginning of my career, stipulating that I should worship the ground Syd Barrett teetered on. The relationship between music writers – cynical, slouched men not given to gratuitous displays of enthusiasm – and Barrett reminded me of something the rapper Ice-T had once said about the relationship between the toughest hip-hop stars and the work of Michael Jackson, an assessment which, though now dim in my mind in its complete form, almost certainly ended with the phrase 'jumping up and down like little bitches'. But while I would quite happily do just that, and several considerably more embarrassing things, in the vicinity of *Thriller* or *Off The Wall*, I couldn't see the appeal of *The Madcap Laughs* or *Barrett* at all.

The hype surrounding Barrett seemed to me a classic case of confusing the legend with the music. For a brief, glittering moment, Syd (real name: Roger) was in possession of one of the psychedelic movement's most productive, kaleidoscopic minds. However, at some point between 1967 and 1969, something (some say Mandrax, some say acid, some say sherbet lemons) had gone very seriously wrong, leaving him an uncommunicative wreck with an inclination to freeze up on stage and rub drugs in his hair. Barrett hadn't just been Pink Floyd's tousle-haired, sylphlike pin-up, he'd been their main songwriter too, and his bandmates had shown immense patience with him, but in 1969 he'd finally edged himself out of the band, going on to make a couple of solo albums and then retreat on a near-permanent basis to the cellar of his mother's house in Cambridge.

Little had been seen of him since, besides a few paparazzi shots, and by the time Peter and I arrived in Cambridge, Barrett's only real competitors for the title of Most Intriguing Rock Recluse were Sly Stone and Brian Wilson – both of whom had also had break-downs in rock's big breakdown era (1967–75), but neither of whom had quite shown the self-discipline of the bona fide hermit. No other living musician generated quite so many rumours: 'Syd hasn't seen daylight for thirty years'; 'Syd is a painter, a gardener'; 'Syd has secret parties with Brian Eno'; 'Syd is diabetic'; 'Syd hangs around my local pub'; 'Syd still thinks he's leader of Pink Floyd'; 'Syd can't spell his first name properly'.

'Over the years, vague bits of information would filter back to me via my mum, who still lives in Cambridge,' Barrett's former bandmate Roger Waters had told me in an interview a few months before my visit to Cambridge. 'That Syd had moved house, or that he had moved back in with his mum, or that he was in the local sanatorium. But I haven't actually spoken to him since 1975.'

During the Seventies, Waters, who'd formed Pink Floyd with Barrett when they were still schoolboys, had gone on with Barrett's replacement Dave Gilmour to turn the band into the prog rock colossus that the majority of the general public knew it as – something which seemed to many an innate contradiction of Barrett's original vision. In 1975, the new, slicker Floyd had made a concept album about their former leader, and, during its conception, Barrett had turned up at the studio, uninvited, eating a bag of boiled sweets and looking virtually unrecognisable. 'He'd put on about four stone and shaved all his body hair,' Waters told me. 'He'd changed from this beautiful curly-haired youth into something resembling the bloke who keeps the scores on that Vic Reeves show.'

There was no denying that the Barrett story was a fascinating one, and you could see why journalists held it close to their heart – for one thing, it allowed the more sharp-minded among them, like Nick Kent, to use witty wordplay such as 'First came the Floyd, then came the void'. But, much as it troubled me to admit it to Peter, the albums quite plainly didn't back it up. If I was honest with myself, I only liked three Barrett songs – 'See Emily Play', 'Interstellar Overdrive' and 'Arnold Layne' – the latter two of which could genuinely piss me off if I had anything even resembling the beginnings of a stress headache. The solo albums, meanwhile, were virtually unlistenable: scrappy, wretched things that I wouldn't feed to my dog if it was starving. For years, having been told in hushed tones by acquaintances that they were 'albums that you just have to have in your collection', I'd pretended to like them, to hear some kind of cracked charm in their meagre fidelity. But then the truth of what I was doing had hit me: I was trying to force some enjoyment out of the sound of a man sitting in an empty room mumbling incoherently about sea creatures while a tape player whirred somewhere in the middle distance. There was nothing musical or endearing about this, just like there would be nothing musical or endearing about me making a Dictaphone recording of my own digestive system.

I wasn't in Cambridge because I was enchanted by Barrett's art; I was in Cambridge because I was enchanted by his legend, or at least my own romanticised version of it, and, in a way, I felt even that was losing its appeal, now I'd stopped pretending that I liked his music. All in all, I wasn't quite sure what Peter and I were looking for – neither in a spiritual sense, nor a physical one. Yet I felt that the search was a necessary stage in Peter's personal musical evolution. Every would-be rock artisan went through a Barrett phase – or something similar – at some point on the way to attaining true manhood. Now was as good a time as any for Peter to get his out of the way.

The only question was: where did we start? My mental picture of Barrett still came from a photograph, taken during the late Sixties, which showed him looking slim, ruffled, kaftaned and tassled. I knew, though, from the photos that had been snatched outside his house in the Eighties, that I should be hunting for something considerably less graceful: a rotund, inelegant, severely balding figure, staring at something at least 3,000 miles behind the camera lens.

'So what you've got to look out for,' I explained to Peter, 'is some kind of cross-fertilisation of Benny from *Crossroads*, Marlon Brando, and the Michael Jackson impersonator from *The Simpsons*.'

'Who's Benny from *Crossroads*?' said Peter.

In truth, I wasn't sure if we *did* want to find Barrett. I had no intention of doorstepping him, and, even if I did have, I wouldn't have wanted to do it with Peter in tow. Instead, I carried with me to Cambridge a nebulous idea of drifting around the city's parks, bike lanes and student bookshops on the off-chance of bumping into him. But I wondered if at root my plan wasn't even vaguer than that. I wanted to meet Syd's 2002 incarnation even less than I wanted to meet Brian Wilson's 2002 incarnation, and I wanted Peter to meet him even less. What I wanted to do was follow the ghost of his twenty-something self (Barrett was, after all, in terms of cult status, the nearest thing to a dead rock star, hence perfectly entitled to his own ghost). I wanted to sit where he had sat, to picture what he had worn, to see the world, just for a moment, the way he had seen it – though not in any psychologically damaging way. Then I wanted to see if Peter could do the same.

'So picture the scene,' I said to Peter, as we sat on the banks of the River Cam, watching a lone punt brave the bracing spring air. 'You're a former maverick songwriter – some would say a genius. But you want to hide from the world indefinitely. You want somewhere sophisticated yet olde worlde, somewhere full of young people, to help give you a preserved sense of youth. Somewhere you can feel like you're still a part of something, but go about your business without being hassled. This seems like the perfect place, doesn't it?'

'I suppose so,' said Peter. 'It's . . . got a lot of good-looking girls.'

'But suppose you're Syd Barrett,' I said. 'Say you're coming here in the mid-Seventies to ponder your lot in life. You've freaked out and left your band, and they've become multi-millionaires, and you're plunged back into obscurity. What would you be thinking?'

'Well, it depends if you're mad or not, doesn't it? I mean, listening to that stuff you had on in the van, I wasn't quite sure. He could have been putting it on.'

'Well, think about both scenarios. What would you think about if you were mad, and what would you think about if you weren't mad?'

'Well, if you were mad, you'd probably be thinking about onions or skirting boards or something. And if you weren't mad . . . well, I guess you'd be thinking about that blonde girl with the rucksack over there.'

'But this is 1974. She wouldn't be here.'

'Her mum might.'

'Good point.'

The two of us stared towards the opposite bank for a moment, lost in thought.

'You know mad people, when they talk really loud on the bus about onions and stuff?' said Peter. 'Have you ever thought what they might do if you talked about onions back to them even louder?'

'Quite frequently, actually.'

'But I bet you've never tried it.'

'No. Never had the guts.'

In the mid-term sun, Cambridge bustled, and Peter and I sucked absent-mindedly on the cola-flavoured laces that I'd purchased from a sweet stall at an outdoor market. It was an easy place in which to let your mind drift. Lecturer-types hurtled past us on wobbly bikes, riding no-handed, gaggles of Japanese students laid out cloths for picnics; the world felt momentarily right, and as we made our way past the majestic façade of King's College, I wouldn't have been surprised if Peter and I had been thinking exactly the same thing: not 'I wonder if we'll find Syd Barrett?' so much as 'Wouldn't this be an ace place to be young?' After a visit to Hot Numbers, a musty second-hand record shop tucked away unusually on a residential street towards the railway line, we'd been directed by the shop's proprietor to the Millpond, a notoriously tranquil corner of the city which, it was rumoured, still provided one of Barrett's favourite pondering spots. But all we'd discovered there were more students, and now we found our attention distracted from Barrett all too easily. Or, at least, I found mine distracted. I wasn't so sure Peter's had been on him in the first place. As we walked across the city, idly taking in the day, every twenty minutes or so I'd hear my impassive friend emit a low grunt. At each of these grunts I'd start slightly and turn round, under the impression that he was talking to me, only to find him muttering insouciantly into his palm-size mobile phone, which was set to vibrate rather than ring (somehow, Peter didn't seem like a ring-tone kind of guy). These conversations were short yet frequent, and would consist solely of words with one syllable, or sometimes less. 'Hi.' 'Yeh.' 'Nnn.' 'Ggg.' 'Cool.' 'Mmm.' 'Tmrrow.' 'Jjj.' 'W.' 'Ha.' 'Sure.' 'See ya.' I could vaguely remember my own self-inflicted problems with communication as a teenager – a particularly recalcitrant 'wounded bison noises' phase surrounding my thirteenth birthday sprang to mind – but even at my most monosyllabic, I'd never spoken in a language remotely like the one Peter was speaking in now. 'At times you may be embarrassed because you may suddenly produce a squeak when you're talking,' Elizabeth Fenwick and Dr Tony Smith had warned teenagers in *Adolescence: The Survival Guide*, but this was something else altogether. Was it really possible to form a meaningful conversation with this few officially recognised words?

I was impressed. Before, I'd imagined that it was only me, Jenny and Ian whom Peter was reticent towards, but, compared to his friends, it was clear that we had it easy.

'What was that about?' I asked him, unable to suppress my curiosity, after he'd clicked the phone shut for the fourth time.

'Just a mate. Wanted some help with this computer game I lent him.'

'What? You mean he couldn't work out how to switch on the console or something?'

'No. There are these samurai bats that you have to get past to get to level six, and he wanted to know how to do it.'

'And you told him how to do it just now?'

He ripped open a bag of pickled-onion-flavour Monster Munch. 'Yeah.'

'But you barely said three words to him.'

'Well, it's pretty simple, once you get the hang of it.'

'Is he a friend you don't like very much?'

'No. That was Quentin – he's totally okay, like really cool.'

The rest of the afternoon had a reassuring pattern to it which, while not quite what I'd hoped for, proved to be a pleasantly laid-back contrast to our encounters with Ed The Troubadour and Brian Wilson. While Peter rumbled into his mobile phone and played Spot The Band T-Shirt, I ogled architecture, browsed in shops selling furniture that I could never afford, and fantasised about a parallel universe where I hadn't dropped out of higher education three months into my first term. Cambridge, while annoyingly tourist-heavy, was undoubtedly a happening city, though not in quite the way I'd imagined. It was the kind of place that you assumed would have more second-hand bookshops, record shops and subterranean hang-outs than it did. The few of these places that were left seemed to be empty or poorly stocked, and the employees, when asked for Barrett gossip, would shrug blankly, or look off into the distance, as if remembering something surprisingly mundane from another lifetime. 'You hear stories,' said a bespectacled man in a tiny, ailing book-shop, which, when I revisited the city a few weeks later, had vanished entirely. 'Stories about him riding his bike by the river. But not so much now. People don't care so much any more.' 'Syd Barrett? No. Is he one of them rappers?' said a man serving in a café, who'd lived in Cambridge since the early Sixties. At least if Barrett had died, like Hendrix or Jim Morrison or Keith Moon or the other cult heroes he was mentioned alongside, he'd have a plaque or some graffiti or a lavish gravestone. As it was, he had nothing – not even the attention of the local population. But perhaps that's the way he'd wanted it all along.

Back on the streets, the academics were heading home to book-lined townhouses and pet cats with names like Kafka and Mailer, the American tourists were asking the hotdog sellers moronic questions ('Does this river, like, lead directly to Oxford? 'Cos that's the next town, right?'), the Japanese girls were folding up their picnic blankets, and, in the bigger gaps between the lot of them, it was possible to spot an unusually large number of men who resembled Benny-from-*Crossroads* two decades on. It was a good city to hide in if you were a spherical man on the runway to old age. It was also a city with great furniture shops, fudge shops, clothes shops and chain stores – a city whose quaintness was preserved via institutions and buildings, rather than gig venues, bohemian eateries or retail outlets. The place seemed somehow beyond Syd Barrett. And while he was surely still here somewhere, painting or being diabetic or hanging out in someone's local pub or having a picnic or gardening or having a secret party with Brian Eno, his ghost had obviously skipped town aeons ago.

REALLY FUNNY (REPRISE)

'It was really funny. There was this party the other week
– at my mate Catherine's? – and for a trick, me and Raf
and Jim – he's like this bloke with a massive head who
everyone calls "Cauliflower" – decided to put pants on
our heads and take a vow of silence for a laugh.'

'I hope they were clean pants. Whose were they?'

'They were Catherine's brother's. He was out. So,
anyway, we're just sitting there in the living room with
these jockey shorts on our heads, and Catherine's mum
comes in early from her yoga class and sees us and
she's like, "What are you doing?", and we're like just
sitting there shrugging, 'cos Raf's said that if any of us
speak or take the pants off our head before midnight
then we have to run around the middle of the road
shouting, "I am the chicken God!" as a penalty.'

'That's quite an elaborate penalty.'

'Yeah. If you knew Raf, you probably wouldn't think
so.'

'So what happened in the end?'

'Yeah, right. It was so cool. In the end, Sophie – that's Catherine's mum? – had picked the phone up and was threatening to call Raf's mum if we carried on not saying anything, and she's just dialled the number when Raf stood up, threw the pants across the room – they landed on this, like, really expensive lamp and it nearly fell off the table – and ran out the door.'

'What, he went home? And left you to talk your way out of it?'

'Yeah, it was kind of okay, though. Sophie's quite cool. We stayed up till about eleven talking about *The Simpsons* and stuff.'

'Do you drink alcohol at these parties?'

'Sometimes. This girl had to have her stomach pumped after this one time. But normally it's not that mad. I don't really drink much 'cos I don't like the taste. And sometimes parents are there anyway.'

'You seem to go to a lot more parties than I went to at your age. I'm jealous. For me it was just the school disco at the leisure centre a couple of times a year. Everyone would go down the off-licence and get shitloads of Special Brew, then we'd watch Johnno Reed – he was a complete nobcheese – snap a load of wing mirrors off cars on the road to school – this was when I was a bit older than you are now, probably fifteen – then we'd go and punch the air to Simple Minds, and get off with people we didn't like. I once got off with this nerdy girl with braces who I pretended I didn't like, but actually did, and called her "Jaws" at school the next day. About four years later I met her again and she was really gorgeous and she said she was going to go out with me, then decided she didn't want to after

all, because of what I'd said about her before. It was
either that or the fact that when I kissed her my Dead
Kennedys hat got in the way. Sorry – I'll shut up. You
probably don't want to hear about that . . .'

'Mmmnff. All sounds . . . weird.'

'Are all your mates' parents really cool and groovy?'

'Not all, but, yeah, most I guess. It's kind of
frustrating.'

'How do you mean? Because you can't rebel against
them?'

'Sort of. I dunno. My dad's always going on about
how much he likes stuff like The Manic Street
Preachers and Rage Against The Machine, but I'm not
sure if he really does.'

'Does he ever shout at you to turn stuff down when
you're at his place?'

'When he's working, sometimes, but not much.'

'What about your mum?'

'Neh. Well . . . I'm not sure. She's kind of cool about
everything. She just worries about my schoolwork,
mostly.'

'How's that going at the moment?'

'Okay, s'ppose. It gets a bit annoying and boring 'cos
with Raf and stuff, he's, like, two years ahead of me,
and his year just don't really do much work, they just
hang around and play guitar and watch all these cool
kung-fu films.'

'But it sounds like quite a laid-back kind of school.
I mean, you have loads of concerts and stuff. I think
my school only had one that was at all rockish. It was
this band Flymow Death, and the Head of Year
stopped it halfway through because all the kids on the

front row were banging their heads against the front of
the stage.'

'Mmm. I guess my school's okay.'

'But you'd rather be on stage somewhere all the
time, playing guitar?'

'Mmnnm.'

'You don't sound too sure.'

'Mmm. No. I am. I'm just tired.'

'Did my cats wake you up in the night?'

'Couple of times, yeah. That one with the weird
voice that goes "eh-weh-weh-weh" and sounds a bit
like a baby.'

'Oh, Brewer.'

'Why's he called Brewer?'

'Well, there's Brewer and there's Shipley, his
brother. They're named after an early Seventies folk
duo. They did this song about pot called "One Toke
Over The Line", but their other stuff is better.'

'What? The cats did a song about pot?'

'Yeah, right. The only pot they'd sing about is the
one with my mum's plant in that they're always pissing in.'

'Would I like them?'

'What? The cats?'

'No. The folk duo.'

'Probably not.'

'Mmm. Yeeeeauuuhhhhhh! So tirrred.'

'Don't worry. We're almost off the motorway now,
then you'll be home in about half an hour. Then I've
got to zoom back and get this van back to Clive.'

'I've been meaning to ask you. Why *are* we travelling
around in a van?'

EDUCATING PETER

LITTLE GREEN FOLKING HOOD

For someone who'd spent much of his adult life avoiding teenagers, I'd developed an unusual amount of theories about them over the years. Naturally, owing to the lack of research to back these theories up, there was every chance that they were complete nonsense, but nevertheless I was happy to have them to cling to. There was, for example, the Modern Teenagers Are The Nastiest Kind Yet theory, which I would adhere to while looking back on my own teenage years and wondering exactly how much of a loathsome little irritant I really was. Then there was the Teenagers Are A Concept Only Meant To Last Five Decades theory, which argued that teenagers were invented in the Fifties but made redundant at the end of the Nineties with the mass-marketing of their rebellion, and gave me a warm sensation of having been in on something good before it became stale. And, finally, there was the closely related Teenagers Don't Have A Proper Subculture Any More theory, which was a convenient way of assuaging any doubts about whether my short-lived phase as part of a 'subversive' indie-rock gang was as significant and energising as it had seemed at the time.

What struck me, unexpectedly, during my adventures with Peter was just how much time I'd spent pondering all this. Throughout my twenties I'd been going innocently about my business, assuming that adolescents were less than a blip on my radar, when in fact some arcane back engine room of my mind – the same back engine room that made such subconscious decisions as 'Yes, it is suddenly true: I don't think *The Doors* is a good movie any more!' – was treating them to the most in-depth analysis. I shiver to reflect on the kind of questions this engine room was posing on an average day, while witnessing me walk along an average high street – 'Did I used to be as obnoxious as that little turd with the bleached hair who's just pushed that granny out of the way in the doorway to Kwik-Save?'; 'Did my Dinosaur Jr t-shirt used to look as crap on me as that goth girl's Puddle Of Mudd t-shirt looks on her?' – when I'd been under the naïve impression that I'd had nothing more probing on my mind than what kind of sausage to buy from the Italian deli and whether there was going to be anything good on Sky Sports that night.

With Peter, the front part of my brain took over and everything began to spew out. How did he compare to me at fourteen? Why did he seem so much more worldly? Did my hair used to be better than his, or worse? Did his parents give him more freedom than mine had given me? Did it work better? Did all my anecdotes used to start with 'It was dead funny', too? Did he see me as someone cool and together, only a little bit older than him, or past it and boring? It was impossible not to dwell on these questions, and, as a result, I could see that I was exasperating him slightly. My tendency to make the same enquiry in seven different ways wasn't fooling him, either.

'So, with the goth thing . . . Let me get this right. It's cool to be goth now? You make lots of friends by going around in white face?'

'Well, yeah, but no, not white face. It's just wearing black, more than anything.'

'What about tight trousers?'

'No. No way. Got to be baggy. Much better. Everyone knows that.'

'You see, that's weird as well. Goth was always about tight trousers in my day. Tight trousers, weird make-up, veils and scary jewellery. It just wasn't cool to be goth – even the alternative kids thought they were weird and depressing. They'd have their weekly night at Rock City in Nottingham and flop their frightening hair around to Fields Of The Nephilim, but apart from that they'd be alone. Then, one day, they all died out. I just assumed they'd all gone to work in banks.'

'Yeah. You told me before.'

Yet, simultaneously, I sensed a breakthrough. By expressing irritation with me, Peter was forced to stop being polite, which gave our relationship a new, looser feeling. I still had my doubts as to whether we were going to be friends when all this was over – between non-relatives, the specific age gap between fourteen and twenty-seven is one that tends not to transcend educational commitments – but at least now we were spending time with each other on a more relaxed basis. No longer did Peter pick up the phone and say, 'Tom who? Oh *that* Tom . . .' or hide in his bedroom for unreasonable amounts of time when I arrived at his house. I started to introduce him to my friends and feel comfortable about it. Occasionally, if I was in London for work purposes, I'd stop in at the Crouch End house for a coffee – not because I felt obliged to owing to my commitment to our project, but because I wanted to. Almost.

As a rainy May turned into a rainier June, I felt that we'd reached a new plateau in our teacher–pupil relationship and that the programme was progressing smoothly. Feedback on my teaching skills was fairly scant from Peter himself, but Jenny reported that the quality of his schoolwork had picked up, and that – though he attempted to disguise it – he tended to return from our adventures in a garrulous mood. On one occasion she'd even overheard him boasting about 'the Hobbit bloke with the axe' to an impressed schoolfriend.

At this point, there was just one hitch in the syllabus, and it revolved around my volunteers – or rather my complete and utter lack of them. I'd half expected this to be the case, but I hadn't anticipated how despondent the reality of the situation would leave me. There was no getting away from it: we were living in a post-Jonathan King age. To most musicians – even eccentric, liberated ones – the thought of hanging around with a bloke and his fourteen-year-old accomplice was a weird one. I could understand, since I thought it was weird as well, but that didn't mean it wasn't frustrating. For entire weeks I emailed my sources, then emailed their sources, asking for an hour or two of their client's time, to little avail. Bono was 'busy', Lenny Kravitz was 'tied up', while Paul McCartney was 'getting married'. These seemed like pretty thin excuses to me, but I soldiered on to what I assumed would be more amenable pastures. Julian Cope, the psychedelic singer-songwriter, said he'd be glad to meet us, particularly after I'd given him the impression that Peter was the reincarnation of Bon Scott from AC/DC, but the loveable Cope's schedule was tight, since he was in the midst of writing a book about stones. Meanwhile, Billy Bragg, the defiantly non-psychedelic singer-wrongwriter, was in the middle of a busy tour schedule and a job teaching guitar at his local school. Others – fire-eating one-man band Rory McLeod, guitar god Norman Blake, former Hawkwind dancer Stacia, Saxon lead singer Biff Byford, the community of famous American blues singers who'd relocated to Yorkshire – were either on the road, out of the country, AWOL, or – least considerately of all – dead. Even Bez, the former Happy Mondays dancer, now fortune-telling for a living under the name 'Mystic Bez', failed to return my call.

It was at times like this that I thanked my lucky stars for the existence of Circulus. In fact, that's not true. I thanked my lucky stars for the existence of Circulus every day of my life; I merely did it more vehemently at times like these.

Now, don't get me wrong here: I'm not hard. And by

the summer of 2002 I was no longer the kind of music fan who'd yell himself stupid sticking up for some band or other. I'd met too many musicians and seen the fragility of too many of my own opinions to view music as a life and death matter. That said, if you were to insult Circulus, I would have done my best to bare-knuckle box the crud out of you on the spot, even if you were Geoff Capes.

Circulus were a folk group from South East London who, since their inception five years previously, I'd come to regard with the level of affection most people reserve for a favourite son. I didn't have a favourite son, which made the whole process easier, but if I had, you could bet he'd have been made aware from an early age that he would be playing second fiddle (or lute, in this case) to Michael, Emma, Robin, Kevin, Leo and Sam. Not only were these six fine musicians in-fluenced by nearly all of my favourite bands – Traffic, Pentangle, Crosby, Stills And Nash, to name just a few – they also wore the kind of Seventies clothes I could never seem to hunt down, and enjoyed the kind of lifestyle I would have loved to live, if only I could have got fully in touch with my inner slacker. Like any good father, I'd watched proudly as they'd experi-mented with facial hair and mind-altering drugs, released limited-edition singles on broom-cupboard record labels, and recruited a small-yet-loyal fanbase of out-of-time dreamers. To me, the fact that they were yet to secure a record deal was one of the great mysteries of the modern world, right up there with Roswell and the continuing gainful employment of Calista Flockhart.

I knew I could count on Circulus. I knew *they* wouldn't find anything untoward about spending a day hanging out with Peter and me. In fact, it's quite possible that if I'd turned up at their house with a small yellow alien life form and said, 'Hi guys! This is Troffimog, from the planet Dustbuster,' the six of them would have simply smiled beatifically, patted us both warmly on the back and stuck the kettle on.

Until a couple of years ago, the founder members of Circulus, Emma Steele and Michael Tyack, had lived on opposite sides of Blackheath, near Greenwich, in South London. The heath itself is a huge, eerie expanse of grass, barely heathlike at all in any conventional sense, abutted by a haunted pub and populated by ravens on a basis too permanent not to be considered ill-omened. I'd lived in a flat overlooking it for twelve months at the start of the Millennium, and always regretted that I hadn't had the chance to use the landscape for anything more profound than the fine-tuning of my golf swing. Despite the introduction of a popular micro-brewery and the regular Saturday night cries of 'Leave it, John! He's not worth it!' that now rang out over the heath's breadth, it was a place which had stubbornly retained its mystique in the face of twentieth- and twenty-first-century progress. It was also a place to which Circulus's music – which, while thriving on the influences of classical West Coast American pop and folk, ultimately seemed steeped in dark, very English history – was irreversibly tied in my head.

That said, the band had recently decided to relocate. I say 'the band' because it's hard not to think of

Circulus as a collective entity, such is the tautness of their personal, sartorial, philosophical and musical bonds. In truth, Emma still lived heathside, in an unruly flat spilling over with ancient fuzz pedals, roach clips and vinyl, but Michael had moved five or six miles down the road to a house in Plumstead, owned by the band's newest members, Kevin and Leo. It was the latter domicile that now provided the group's base.

My trip to Plumstead with Peter marked my first visit to the new Circulus headquarters, and the house was everything I'd expected it to be and more. I'd wanted Peter to see a proper musician's dwelling, where every fibre spoke of the residents' undying commitment to Sergeant Rock – or Sergeant Acid Folk Rock, in this case – and everything that surrounded him, and here was the real thing. Mr Benn would have been impressed: the magical threshold in his favourite fancy dress shop had nothing on the one that separated the interior of Camp Circulus from the humdrum street outside. Inside were more rugs and drapes than you'd find in the most overstocked souk, odd little wicker heads and odder little wicker men, Buck Rogers-evoking half-moon speakers attached to the kind of stereo system you saw advertised in Seventies issues of *Rolling Stone*, a cat called Orbit, and a recording room that looked like it had been stolen from *The Old Grey Whistle Test*. If you ignored a poster advertising a Demis Roussos comeback tour, all evidence of post-1976 history had been banished.

Only one piece of the picture was missing.

'Where are the records?' I asked, and with a

conspiratorial smirk Kevin and Michael unhooked a couple of drawing pins and let a huge, room-size batik hanging fall away from the wall. Except it wasn't a wall made of bricks, but vinyl.

'There were about two hundred thousand at one stage,' said Michael. 'I think there are a few less than that now. Kevin used to work in a warehouse and get them free.'

'A *good* warehouse,' said Kevin.

In a place like this it was easy to get distracted from the itinerary of the day, and time briefly stood still as I reeled slightly. The names flashed before my eyes in a blur – BrewerAndShipleyEastOfEdenCOBStone AngelMightyBabyFreshMaggotsPentangle MellowCandleSunforestAstralNavigations – every cult hippie-era band I'd ever loved, and every cult hippie-era band I wanted to love. I had an urge to bathe in vinyl, or at least to lie on a bed and roll in it in that way that people do with money in films about gambling. It took me a moment to remember that I was a recovering vinyl junkie who wasn't supposed to dribble in the presence of records any more, by which point Michael and Kevin had disappeared downstairs. It took me another moment to realise that Peter was standing behind me, his head at a slight angle. He was looking at me in the way you might look at an overweight kid who's been given free rein in a sweet shop.

'Have you ever seen anything like this?' I asked him.

'No. Never.'

'I mean . . . it's just – everything.'

'Well, not everything. I mean, I bet he doesn't have *Cruelty And The Beast* by Cradle Of Filth.'

'I don't think that came out on vinyl.'

Typically, the previous night – a Friday – had seen a party at Circulus HQ, and the acrid weed cloud that served as the band's perennial halo was even more (omni)potent than usual. I'd felt stoned almost as soon as I'd mounted the stairs, and I worried about Peter, since I didn't know how lenient Jenny was about this sort of exposure. Maybe *she* still smoked weed, maybe she did it in front of Peter, maybe she wouldn't dream of doing either. Perhaps Peter had already smoked it himself. Fourteen-year-olds were pretty advanced these days, weren't they? Once again, it was dawning on me how little I knew about contemporary parenthood. But, not wishing to take any risks, we headed out to the garden, stumbling through an ash-caked kitchen and a room decorated entirely in mirrored cardboard, and skirting around slumped survivors from the previous night's debauchery.

Outside, lunch was being served – a charred tray of that specific kind of oven chips that seem to have flour, rather than potato, as their centre – and proper introductions were made. Here, finally, was the chance for Peter to hang out with musicians as you might hang out with friends, and I felt proud as I introduced my six retrograde heroes. There was Michael, for whom the word 'easy-going' had been invented, for whom there were never enough medieval capes in the world, and for whose looks a new hippie James Bond movie villain needed desperately to be invented. There was dark and mysterious Robin, otherwise known as 'The Walking Cheekbones'. There was Emma, the angelic vocalist with the cheeky edge.

There was Kevin, who liked to wear wigs. And there were Leo and Sam, who, if I was truly honest with myself, I hadn't got to know particularly well.

Within no time at all, Peter had helped himself to a powdery charcoal chipette and been sucked into a discussion about guitars with Michael and Robin.

'So you're into Flugelphones, then? We generally prefer something with a bit more give, like a B Pierce Flinbacker.'

'Cool. Yeah, I like the Flinbacker. But I just tried a Swugelbacker Airbus. It's not so good on feedback, but you should hear it, like, *chime.*'

'Yeah? Swugelbacker made a wicked Airbus in about '73 – a bad momma. Hard to find now, but you should look out for it. A bit like the Swerving Zed that McCracken made in '78, but more solid in the impact area.'

'Oh. McCracken? Have you ever seen one of their Flying Whores? My mate Raf's always on about them.'

The previous night I'd been in bed by ten, after a History channel documentary, a chicken salad and a lone bottle of organic beer, but now I got the hazy, elated feeling that I, too, had been living it up in the House Of Folk. Circulus had an effortless way of drawing you in to their mindset and their psychic powers seemed to be working on Peter, who, from the moment we entered the house, had instantly seemed more relaxed than I'd ever seen him. As he talked shop with Circulus's rhythm section, I found myself momentarily free of my caretaker responsibilities and took the opportunity to soak up the rare afternoon sun and entertain Orbit with a stray mandolin string. I hoped, for my hand's sake, that it wasn't the kind made from cat gut, but soon got the impression that Orbit wouldn't kick up a fuss if it was. Even Circulus's pets seemed sort of stoned and groovy.

This, I thought, was The Life. Being in a band wasn't about hotel rooms or signing sessions or fashion shoots; it was about being able to sit in your back garden together and talk rubbish all day. Circulus didn't have a record deal, never had any money, spent much of their life on the dole, yet they were the happiest people I knew. The skinniest people I knew, but the happiest. Wherever they went, flares, capes, outlandish headwear and laughter followed. And whatever happened for the remainder of the day, I felt sure Peter could take something positive away from this experience. After all, the kid hadn't exactly had an easy introduction to the rock and roll life: he'd met an axe-wielding busker, hung out at a petrol station, stared into a closed waxwork museum, got stuck in a lift with a frustrated mime artist, and chased the ghost of a cult icon his tutor wasn't even interested in. He needed a break. And he wasn't the only one. As I looked across the grass at my for-once keen-eyed pupil, I felt the lull of driving fatigue, sun and safety kick in, and drifted off into a contented half-sleep. Around me, four or five conversations continued, flitting in and out of my dream-like state . . .

'Their first album, or the second, with the scarecrow on the cover?'

'He sucks.'

'No, it's an Epiphone, I think.'

'Carrot soufflé! Woo-hoo.'

'He's mad on chips. I don't know what it is. Is that weird for cats? Crisps, too. But only smoky bacon.'

'No, I only met him a few months ago. But he's known my mum for ages. This whole thing was kind of her idea.'

'Yeah, no, the first, with the bear.'

'Our other cat, Rameses, prefers Twiglets.'

'What about carrots? We've got loads in the kitchen.'

'Do you think it will fly if you attach it with this piece of string?'

'Ha! Wicked!'

'*You dirty old man!*'

It was the last voice that prompted me to bolt awake. It had a Smurf-like quality to it – a 45rpm pace in sharp contrast to everyone else's 33rpm. It was hard to tell how long I'd been asleep. Under an hour, I sensed, but as I surveyed how our little garden party had progressed, it felt like at least a couple of days. To my right, Michael, watched by Emma and Robin, was alternately inhaling, shouting, and inflating balloons from a helium canister. To his left, Leo and two of the slumped survivors who'd been around the kitchen table earlier were attaching carrots and chips to the bottom of other balloons with string. Meanwhile, over on an old sofa, beneath the shade of a holly bush, Kevin was showing Peter the correct stance and grip for the firing of a gun.

'Morning, Tom,' said Emma. 'We're shooting balloons. Want to join in?'

'Is that . . . Is that a real gun?' I said, rubbing my eyes.

'No,' said Peter. 'Just an air gun. It's Kevin's. The

idea is to chop the carrot down just small enough for the balloon to carry it, then let it go and shoot it. Cool or what?'

'Er . . . yeah. Be careful.'

Over the previous seven years, I'd interviewed two or three hundred musicians. Some had claimed to drink whisky for breakfast; some had claimed to be the reincarnation of Jesus Christ; others had claimed to be clairvoyant preachers in league with the devil. I'd lain flat on the roofs of skyscrapers and stared at the New York skyline with some; I'd hung out at Stonehenge with others. But never had I come close to shooting carrot-carrying balloons with any of them. Somehow, this fact struck me as hugely significant. Had I wasted my young life? Perhaps. And now it was too late. I was too busy being a responsible father figure to join in.

'I mean, y'know,' I continued, 'that thing looks dangerous. Watch it. Seriously. What if it, y'know, twists in your hand when you shoot it?'

'I'm okay.'

Bang!

'See?'

'Mmm. Good shot.'

'Wanna go?'

'No. I'll just sit here and eat my chips.'

'Suit yourself.'

And so the afternoon progressed. It was hard to find fault with Circulus, and in the half-decade I'd known them, I'd only located one flaw in their friendship. Actually, 'flaw' was too strong a word; it was more of an irksome discrepancy between their plane of existence and the rest of the world's. It was known, to all those who walked in the band's social circle but held down conventional full-time jobs, as Circulus Meantime. Circulus Meantime, which originated a couple of miles south of Greenwich observatory, was a bit like Greenwich Meantime, but with minutes that lasted ninety-eight seconds instead of the usual sixty. Circulus Meantime wasn't merely about being late; it was about being punctually late. Circulus Meantime wasn't about frequently staying in bed beyond eleven am; it was about *always* staying in bed beyond eleven am, and showing *discipline* about it. There were times in the past – social occasions like my twenty-fifth birthday, during which the band had arrived through the pub door just as I was staggering out of it – when the conventions of this different time zone could be frustrating, but over the years I'd learned to allow for it. It was surprisingly easy, once you worked out the ten commandments.

1. Thou shalt not turn up at a pub before last orders.
2. Thou shalt not say, 'Shall we go?' Thou shalt let it happen, like, organically.
3. Thou shalt stay up late enough to watch the sun rise at least twice a week.
4. Thou shalt not deem it fashionable to be late. Thou shalt deem it *altruistic*.
5. Thou shalt never let thy train timetable stand in the way of sartorial perfection.
6. Thou shalt not leave thy joint half-finished.
7. Thou shalt not forget thy cape.
8. Thou shalt let thy platter of ancient tunes spin to its natural end.

9. Thou shalt never hang around during that dead, desolate period after the shops shut and before the pubs fill up.

10. Thou shalt amble.

This afternoon was a classic example of Circulus Meantime. The idea had been to head up to the nearby Oxley's Wood to shoot the band's first pop video, but the garden party had become a bit like the party in *Buffy The Vampire Slayer* where the Vengeance Demon grants Buffy's sister's wish that no-one ever leave. On the one hand, I wished I could spend more Saturday afternoons like this. On the other, the eight of us had other, bigger plans for the day, and I had a responsibility to return Peter to Crouch End in time for his fencing class.

'Shall we go then, guys?' I announced, trying to sound as casual as possible, but somehow feeling like the biggest square in Plumstead.

'Groan,' said the garden.

Eventually, capes were donned, acoustic musical equipment was gathered and scrawny legs creaked into action. We were to travel in convoy: half of us in Alice, Michael's Seventies Ford Escort, the other half with me in the Ford Focus. I'd put the van into retirement for the time being, having been intimidated by the you're-a-weirdo-aren't-you nature of the looks Clive The Assistant Haulage Executive had been giving me upon my returns to the depot, but now, as I saw Circulus's collection of props, I began to regret it. Considering Circulus were always broke, their rate of gadget-acquisition was astounding. When I walked into a charity shop, I found endless Barbara Taylor Bradford novels, *Music For Pleasure* albums and rejected Littlewoods clothing for the old beige pensioner market. When Michael, Robin and Emma did exactly the same thing, they unearthed a treasure trove of retro audio gold and bohemian finery. Now, as I dropped hints with my accelerator pedal and watched the metal and cloth pile up in my rear-view mirror, I wondered what my friends were expecting and precisely how long our project would take to complete.

Oxley's Wood on a Saturday was full of golden retrievers, cyclists and small children with ice-cream beards. It was a bit like many other suburban British parks, but more mystical – although whether it would have been as mystical without Circulus there was hard to say. The band had a way of invading and altering a place with their presence. They didn't dress so differently from Ed The Troubadour, but while people whispered and pointed towards Ed, they simply grinned at Circulus and wanted to join in.

Kevin was the first to climb the big oak tree – the biggest, perhaps, in the entire park – and others quickly followed: Michael, Emma, Leo and a zealous-looking Peter. Robin operated the video camera. I, meanwhile, lingered at the bottom of the trunk, passing instruments up to my friends, guarding the ghetto blaster and scribbling in my notebook. On the ghetto blaster, a country and western song about chicken by Sunforest rang out above the trees. In the tree, though, the only things being plucked were guitars and mandolins. On bongos, Peter, now in a fetching Lincoln green hooded cape, joined the groove and explored his 'tribal' side. Every few minutes, a confused cyclist or enchanted child would stop and wonder what in the name of Beelzebub these bizarrely attractive people who dressed like elves were up to. Then they'd pause and their faces would no longer express confusion, but wistful wonder, a look which said nothing so much as 'Why don't I know people who do stuff like this in their spare time?' It was the sort of scene that it was an honour to be part of – the true essence of creativity.

I was creating as well, or at least trying to. As designated director of the video, it was my job to come up with a concept and storyboard. The idea was to do this spontaneously. My problem was Sunforest's chicken song. It was hard to get it out of my head. Every theme I came up with seemed to have chickens in it, either a) crossing a road, b) getting decked by one of Bernard Matthews' turkeys, or c) taking LSD. Circulus hadn't written the song for this video yet, but I was pretty sure that what they did write wouldn't involve fowl.

Eventually, I came up with a story – a reworking of the Little Red Riding Hood myth. Little Green Folking Hood (Peter), while on the way to his grandma's house across the park in Woolwich, carrying a bag of normal mushrooms, would be abducted by a coven of strange, chanting folk musicians (Circulus – or, as they would be known here, The Evil But Really Quite Gentle Pixie People), who would force him to eat their evil mushrooms. First, he would escape, aided by the strong and silent Folkie With No Name (me), but, finally, in a stunt which involved one of The Evil But Really Quite Gentle Pixie People (Kevin) posing as a holly bush, he would find himself ensnared for eternity. The final scene would depict him being led away to a quiet corner and offered a selection of weeds (non-hallucinogenic) in an ancient ritual that I hadn't quite worked out the point of. The film would serve as a cautionary tale concerning the debasing effects of too many vegetables on the nation's youth. It wasn't going to be *The Godfather*, but, considering the whole thing had taken me six and a half minutes to write, I was proud of it.

'Sounds alright,' said Peter.

'Can we wear capes?' said Michael.

'Where do we get the mushrooms?' said Emma.

Moving on to a path overlooking a walled garden, we began filming – first a heavy-breathing, running scene along the path, then the first encounter between Little Green Folking Hood and The Evil But Really Quite Gentle Pixie People in the garden. From beneath a nearby tree, Kevin located some grey fungus which would pass adequately for mushrooms. A rotting park bench, emblazoned with the legend 'Tozza dun Kelly Anne here – 11.4.1998', served as my director's chair (I wondered if Kelly and Anne were two different people). From here I barked instructions to my cast such as 'Try and suffer *with* the mushrooms, Peter' and 'Emma, dahling, *sense* his pain with your upper forehead', then, seeing that they could handle themselves perfectly well without me, amused myself by trying on a selection of Michael's hats and capes. Occasionally a passing man in a tracksuit would wander into the background of the shot, but progress was smooth. Peter, who'd obviously studied drama at school, had an unusually intense way of gazing into the camera, while Robin, on camera duty, was clearly from the Scorsese school of tracking shots, and, as darkness swept in over the woods, we had a wrap. Or, to look at it another way, a rush job. In roughly a month's time we'd reconvene, by which point Circulus would have edited these images into some semi-coherent form and placed their spooky, warped folk melodies alongside them.

Before I hurried Peter back to his fencing instructor in North London, there was just time to view 'the dailies' back at The House Of Folk, as Emma made me a quick VHS copy of our work. I wasn't sure if you could still call your dailies 'dailies' when you were only shooting for one day in total, but I did so anyway, since it made me feel professional. I needed to feel professional. Maybe it was too early to ascertain if what we'd created was genius or crud, but I was leaning towards crud. Circulus themselves seemed quite content with it, but, then again, the only home video of theirs that I'd seen before was their 'cover version' of *Permissive*, the long-lost, indescribably grimy movie about bitchiness and suicide in the groupie underworld of Seventies rock. This was three minutes long and consisted entirely of Michael trying on wigs, repeatedly holding up a card with 'London, 1971' written on it, and shouting at Emma to get out of the bath.

It was only later, watching the *Little Green Folking*

Hood tape for a second time at home, with the help of the fast forward and rewind buttons, that I noticed Peter – rear frame, taking advantage of a break in the action – sneakily slipping a Blue Oyster Cult CD into the pocket of my shoulder bag.

I'd initially thought it was a mushroom.

EDUCATING PETER

A SPIRITUAL BEARD

'We seem to be meeting a lot of people who wear capes.'

'Yeah. It's funny that. I used to like capes when I was a kid – perhaps it's something to do with that. I had this one that my mum sewed for me: it had a "T" for Tom on it, in the same way Superman's had an "S". Did you ever wear capes when you were younger?'

'Um. Not really.'

'But they're quite goth, aren't they? I mean, Batman – isn't he a bit of a goth icon?'

'No! No way.'

'But you enjoyed wearing that green cape, didn't you? Don't deny it.'

'Yeah. It was fun. But I was glad to get my jacket back on. We miss each other if we're apart too long. But they were so cool, those guys. Like, really mental, but dead nice.'

'Yeah. I always find myself doing an unusual amount of giggling when I'm with them, but can never really remember what was funny.'

'Mmm. But, yeah, what I mean is, though, we seem to be doing a lot of folk stuff. I suppose those guys weren't folk, like in the way the stuff my Uncle Charles – he's like this hey nonny nonny guy with a beard – listens to, but they sort of were.'

'Well, I think you find far more interesting people in folk music, most of the time, than you find in ordinary rock music. You never get a folk musician talking about indie bonuses.'

'What's an indie bonus?'

'It's this term that stems from all these indie bands in the Nineties who used to say, "We just do what we do, and if anyone else likes it, it's a bonus." It's like the ultimate boring thing to say in an interview.'

'What? You mean a bit like when they say, "The music should speak for itself." '

'Yeah. A bit. But what I was saying is folk musicians nearly always have an interesting story, because their music's so inextricably linked to people and places. It's not just this faceless, bland thing. Also, most of the best rock has its roots in folk. Led Zeppelin are very folk in a way. But don't worry – we're only meeting a couple more folkies.'

'Are they hey nonny nonny guys with beards?'

'One of them is, sort of. Although he's more hey beery beery than hey nonny nonny. The other one's got a kind of spiritual beard.'

'Oh-oh.'

'And there's a really important album I want you to listen to which is sort of folk, but Seventies rock people liked it.'

'Does it have songs about thyme and roses on it?'

'Er . . . A few.'

'I don't mind. It's not that. It's just . . . I was wondering if we could do something that involved something a bit heavier. Something a bit, y'know, punk. Maybe.'

'Well, I dunno. I don't have much contact with punk people these days. I'm a bit scared of them, to be honest. I used to be well into the whole scene, though.'

'Really? I wouldn't have guessed.'

'I'll have to show you the pictures some time. Or maybe I won't. It was a weird phase: lots of cut-off golf trousers and friends with names like Zac and Thud. I still have some of the bruises to prove it.'

'Really?'

'No. I was bullshitting. Bruises don't last ten years.'

'The whole thing's just kind of hard to imagine.'

'Why?'

'I dunno. Just . . . Did you have a band?'

'Yeah. Of course. I sang . . .'

'You sang! Ha!'

'I dunno why it's so funny. Listen. Tell you what. I'll tell you a story, then you might understand a bit better. Then you can tell me a story about one of your bands.'

'Ur. Okay. Go on then.'

'No. I'm going to write it down.'

'What, now?'

'No. I'm driving.'

'Oh yeah.'

'To get inside this story, you're going to have to imagine a world with no Slipknot. A world where not every city had a Starbucks on every third street. A world where mobile phones were the size of dictionaries . . .'

'I think I get the picture.'

'. . . A world where Kurt Cobain hadn't shot himself yet.'

'Cooooool!'

'I'm going to put it in the present tense.'

'Why?'

'So you can imagine you were there more easily.'

'Oh.'

'The story starts in a recording studio, where the microphones smell.'

'I hate the way they do that.'

EDUCATING PETER

TOM'S STORY

Matt is sitting on the amplifier, reading from a sheet of A4 paper. I'm leaning against the wall, examining my nails for something non-existent, in that way that people do when they're feeling simultaneously bored and smug. Matt looks up and shakes his head. A smile spreads across his face – a bit like the one you imagine Jagger might have flashed Richards upon receipt of the riff to 'Satisfaction'. 'This is it,' he tells me. 'This . . . this is the greatest thing you've ever written.'

It's 1993, and Matt and I are the principal song-writers in Rick Argues, the punk band we have formed at FE college. That is to say, I bring four verses and a chorus of preternaturally banal teen angst to the studio, and Matt constructs a three-chord riff around them in the style – we would like to think – of our Californian teen punk heroes, Green Day. Either that or we just cover a Green Day song. Green Day are still in the hardcore punk ghetto at this point, and have yet to be signed to Warner Music. We look at it this way:

liking them makes us very obscure and cool, and if, when we finally get around to playing a gig, someone mistakes one of Green Day's songs for one of ours, we won't go out of our way to correct them.

Matt listens exclusively to three-chord punk music. I listen exclusively to three-chord punk music and The Smiths. I think The Smiths are brilliant. Matt thinks they are 'puff music, for puffs', even though Matt – who, incidentally, won't be homophobic for ever – has never properly heard The Smiths. Matt and I argue about The Smiths constantly, but try to meet some-where in the middle (i.e. I am banned from mentioning The Smiths, Morrissey, ambiguous sexuality, or our college friend, Robin Smith). But today, after three months of hard work, Matt is looking at me affection-ately, concluding we have made a major breakthrough. This, I can tell he is thinking from the far-off look in his eyes, is the first step on the way to a support tour with our peers, Throaty Toad, a local band with the distinction of 'once going out for a drink with the Buzzcocks'.

What is the inspiration behind Rick Argues? I don't think either of us can quite put our finger on it. I would ask John and Joe, the other two members of our band, what they thought, but it would probably be a waste of time. John, who drums, and Joe, who plays bass, are never quick to take advantage of Rick Argues' democratic forum for free expression.

'I was thinking of moving the second line of verse one into the third line of verse two. What do you think, John?' I sometimes ask John.

'Okay,' John replies.

'What do you think of this riff?' Matt sometimes asks John.

'S'alright,' John says.

In an attempt to get John more involved, I write 'John's Hair', a song built around the central refrain 'Once it was short/Now it is long', detailing the journey of his lustrous locks from crewcut to pony tail. 'What do you think, John?' I ask.

'S'alright,' says John.

Joe, our bassist, isn't quite so loquacious. One of life's great smilers, Joe has such a repertoire of attentive grins that it's possible to have a half-hour conversation with him without realising he hasn't spoken. When Matt and I fight over The Smiths, Joe grins. When Matt tells me that what I've written is soppy shite, Joe grins. When I gently suggest to Matt that he might want to add a fourth chord to his repertoire, Joe grins. Joe's grins, despite their diversity, all seem to mean the same thing: 'S'alright'. Do John and Joe enjoy being in Rick Argues? Who knows. Do John and Joe talk about Matt and me behind our backs? Perhaps, but in our presence they communicate with one another on a purely psychic level.

On the days we can't afford a proper rehearsal room, I drive across town to Matt's front room. First of all, though, I pick up John and Joe, who live on the posh side of town, and load their equipment into the boot of my parents' Vauxhall Astra. I drive in the style of a punk rock Alain Prost, but not quite as slowly. I am an idiot. No-one talks, because I've worked out by now that John and Joe are beyond words, and besides, Green Day's *Kerplunk!*, cranked up on the car stereo, makes conversation difficult. You might say that, as seventeen-year-olds go, I'm a reckless driver, but I know the etiquette of the highway. When, such as now, I detect the wail of an ambulance's siren behind me, I pull over to the side of the road with my hazard flashers on. Only, instead of an ambulance, the Astra is surrounded by three police cars, one in front, one at the back and one at the side.

Joe, John and I are bundled roughly out of the Astra and get a police car each. I see John's policeman accidentally-on-purpose trap John's leg in the door. For once, John doesn't say, 'S'alright.' He says, 'Owwww!!' The policeman doesn't apologise.

My policeman doesn't say anything for a couple of minutes, while I sit there, thinking how much he looks like a human version of Basil Brush. He asks me for my name and licence, then enquires what I was doing outside Joe's house five minutes ago. I tell him I was picking Joe up. He asks me where we are going. I tell him our band, Rick Argues, is on the way to rehearse our new song, 'T-Shirt'.

Basil asks me a few more questions, about where I live, how old I am. Then he makes a call via his crackly radio. By this point, his two colleagues are standing outside the car, waiting to talk to him. Joe and John are sitting on the grass verge; Joe looks sad and worried, but is still sort of grinning.

It is clear there has been a terrible mistake. We have been reported by one of Joe's neighbours for breaking into Joe's house and stealing Joe's bass guitar and amplifier. Basil returns to the car and explains this to me in the chuntering voice of the six-year-old who knows he is wrong for setting fire to the manger in the school nativity play but doesn't want to admit it in the presence of his tough mates.

'If you're going to have to pick Joe up in the future, just be more careful next time you're in his area,' Basil tells me.

I wonder what Basil means by this. How can we be more careful to show Joe's neighbours we aren't breaking into his house? Perhaps I should refrain from driving a nine-year-old car with a Dead Kennedys logo painted on the side, or, even better, we should all wear fluorescent t-shirts with name tags and 'Law-Abiding Citizen' emblazoned on them. I am about to put this suggestion to Basil, but think better of it.

'And there's one other thing,' he says. 'You went through a red light back there.'

'It was amber,' I correct him.

'It's the same thing.'

I really have to put Basil right here, if only for his own good and his future as a successful policeman. 'How can they be the same thing if one's orange and the other one's red?'

'Both signals request the driver to stop. I'm going to let you out the car now, but just remember: you've been very lucky not to be fined. It's a criminal offence to waste police time, you know.'

Police time? What about Rick Argues' time?

We arrive at Matt's place in stunned silence. For once, though, I feel I can rely on John and Joe for support: we're all pretty shaken up, right? Those pigs are such bastards, aren't they? We're innocent punk rock heroes, railing against the system! I recount the experience to Matt, being careful to double the number of police cars and the level of physical violence.

'So then this bastard copper slams John's head against the car bonnet and starts reading him his rights!' I tell Matt.

'Fucker told me I sped through a red light at ninety miles an hour. I told him where to stick it!' I tell Matt.

I look to John and Joe for support.

'S'right,' says John.

'. . .' says Joe, grinning.

Rick Argues' signature song is called 'T-Shirt'. I genuinely feel it's my masterpiece. Here is the first verse:

> Over there you are
> Walking in the dark
> I don't know your name
> But I know your name

The bridge builds the tempo slightly:

> I'd like to thank you
> For your T-shirt
> Congra-tu-lations
> On your T-shirt

The chorus goes like this:

> T-shirt, T-shirt, I remember
> T-shirt, T-shirt, last December
> T-shirt, T-shirt, look but don't touch
> T-shirt, T-shirt, I've seen too much

I like the coda best, though:

> Don't throw it away!
> Don't throw it away!
> Don't throw it away!

'T-Shirt' is intended to be a meaningful commentary on the eternal search for identity via band logos among indie youth at Nottingham's premier alternative venue, Rock City. Through its more profound lyrics – 'I don't know your name/But I know your name' – I am trying to convey the sensation of not knowing someone, but feeling like you know someone. Ultimately, though, the song is a love letter to the girl in the Suede t-shirt I see at Rock City every week, who, on the one occasion that I tried to speak to her, told me to 'piss off' before I'd even managed to say hello. One day, I hope, she will sit in the front row at a Rick Argues gig, and I will be able to sing our signature song to her. As I said, I am an idiot.

Rick Argues are called Rick Argues because we have a friend, Rick, who argues. We invite Rick along to our rehearsals as our mascot, but he just disrupts the creative process by arguing.

'Why did you call yourselves Rick Argues?' asks Rick.

'Because you argue a lot,' Matt and I tell him.

'No, I don't,' argues Rick.

Rick argues about everything, but doesn't seem to realise it. I've noticed that when I abruptly change my mind and agree with him on a topic over which I previously disagreed with him, he'll drop his original argument and borrow my original argument, just because he likes arguing so much. I don't think Rick has ever agreed with anyone in their presence.

Matt and I have a song called 'Rick Argues', too. It doesn't have a chorus, and the verses simply consist of me shouting out random topics which I've argued about (apart from The Smiths, of course, who are banned). For example:

> Argued about my mum
> Argued about my leg
> Argued about John Major
> Argued about hedgeclippers
> Argued about third division footballers
> It makes me happy!

We don't think of it as one of our classics.

The microphones in the rehearsal rooms where Rick Argues practise smell of regurgitated parmesan. The crusty who owns the studios, Chiz, usually sits in the room adjacent to the room where Rick Argues rehearse, reading the *Daily Star*, smoking weed and feeding Kentucky Fried Chicken to his dog, KFC. 'Here, KFC, want some KFC?' enquires Chiz.

'Wuff!' replies KFC.

Our plan was to spend six months honing our style before cutting a demo or playing a gig. However, we feel, with our polished version of 'T-Shirt' and a new song, 'Bike Mother (I Want Your Omelette)', we are ready to book time in the Big Room, where people record things.

'Chiz, we want to cut a demo,' Matt and I inform Chiz.

'Are you sure?' asks Chiz.

We eventually convince him that we're ready to lay down some tracks, and we're booked in for the following Monday. When we arrive, though, Chiz claims he has double-booked us. The week after that, Chiz tells us his mixing desk is playing up. He sends us back to the rehearsal room with a small, early 1980s tape recorder and a C90 cassette. Matt and I see the rehearsal through in a dolorous mood, both of us thinking the same thing, but not wanting to say it.

'Matt, do you think we're actually any good?' I ask Matt the next day at college.

'Of course we are,' Matt replies.

'But, y'know, I mean proper good. Like on-tour-with-Green-Day good.'

'I've told you, "T-Shirt" could quite easily be off *Kerplunk!*'

'So when I sing it back to back with a Green Day song, it sounds just the same?'

'Yeah.'

'And that's all we want, really, isn't it?'

'Yeah.'

I've never wanted to be a rock star – I just want to meet the girl with the Suede t-shirt (I am an idiot). Matt doesn't want to be a rock star, either, but he has different reasons, chief of them being that rock stars are corporate scum. I think if Matt could bring himself to admit it to his subconscious, he would *really* like to be a rock star. I would like to be in a band, definitely, but

I don't think I'm particularly musical. I've thought about the band I want to be in, and I think it should have horns and mandolins and lyrics about nothing in particular and everything in the world, all at once. It should be gentle and poetic, or epic and surreal, not laconic and primitive. Matt would kill me if he knew.

Matt calls me up one night. 'Up for a rehearsal this weekend?'

'Yeah, deffo,' I say. I'm panicking because droning away in the background as I speak is *Bona Drag*, a solo album by Morrissey.

When I come to college in a t-shirt which doesn't say 'Too Drunk To Fuck', 'Never Mind The Bollocks' or 'I Am Not What I Own', Matt tells me off. 'What the fuck you wearing that for?' he asks me when I turn up in the bootleg Teenage Fanclub shirt I bought outside Rock City the night before. I'm growing my hair out slightly, and hoping he hasn't noticed. At lunchtime, in the college refectory, I often think I'd quite like to sit next to Nick and Steve from my design class, but they have long hair, and Matt says all people with long hair are 'townies' or 'hippies'. Matt also says you can't trust a song which doesn't include swearing. The few lyrics Matt writes for Rick Argues invariably contain the words 'coagulate', 'enema' and 'pigfuck'.

I think I'm in the process of re-evaluating my artistic relationship with Matt.

'. . . This is the greatest thing you've ever written,' Matt is repeating, still shaking his head at the piece of A4. 'I mean it. This is it, Tom. This is what I knew you had in you.'

John fiddles with his drumsticks. Joe grins. I slouch

against the wall, shrug, and smile internally. I'm wasting more of Rick Argues' time, but I have to admit I'm quite enjoying this. Maybe I'll let Matt construct a few chords around my lyrics. Then, at some point, I'll gently explain to him that the words on the piece of paper are not mine, that I copied them this morning from the sleeve of The Smiths' 1983 album, *Hatful Of Hollow*. But not yet. Not just yet.

EDUCATING

BIG KYLIE MINOGUE FAN

PETER

'What happened after that?'

'Oh. We split up.'

'What? Without playing a gig?'

'Yeah. We were meant to play the college refectory one time, but the computer room above it flooded so the gig got cancelled.'

'That's a bit shit. Can you call yourself a proper band if you haven't played a gig?'

'The Beatles went four years without playing a gig, so, yeah. Can Goat Hero call themselves a proper band if you haven't recorded a demo?'

'We're just getting properly prepared. Anyway, it's Punishment again now.'

'What? Why did you change it back?'

'Raf got bitten by a goat at breaktime.'

'Ouch.'

'So what happened to Matt? Do you still know him?'

'Yeah. He's one of my best mates. He works at the DSS these days. Big Kylie Minogue fan.'

'What about Rick?'

'You could say we've grown apart. He argued too much. Works for New Labour now.'

'I hate Labour. It totally pisses me off what they're doing with A-levels.'

'Mmm. Don't tell Rick that. I have a feeling he'd be forced to argue.'

'What about the girl in the t-shirt song?'

'I went out with her for six and a half years.'

'Did she ever hear the demo?'

'No. Joe stole it.'

'I can't believe you liked Green Day.'

'Sad, isn't it?'

'Well . . . I'm sorry, but yeah. They're a dork's band.'

'Your turn then.'

'What? You want me to write it down too?'

'No. I don't imagine you'd ever get around to it, seeing how long it's taking you to read that Julian Cope book.'

'No. I probably wouldn't.'

'Go on then . . .'

'Just let me think for a moment . . .'

REALLY FUNNY (REPRISE AGAIN BUT A BIT LONGER)

'It was really funny. There was Raf and me, and we were standing outside class, waiting for this kid, Jeff, who was supposed to be lending Raf his homework to copy, and this girl Carly walked past and this piece of paper dropped out of her bag. Raf picked it up and it was, like, this love letter . . . No. Hold on.'

'What?'

'That story's a bit shit.'

'Sounded quite interesting to me.'

'No. It's, er . . . I better not tell you that. Let me think of another. Hold on a moment . . .

'Okay. I know. It was dead funny. Me, Raf and these two mates of ours, Zed and Nic, were in central London one day and we decided to ride the Circle Line all the way round for a laugh. Anyway, that got a bit boring after a while, and there was this, like, really tall building in Kensington, and Raf decided . . . No, I can't believe I'm telling you this. It's so stupid.'

'No. Carry on. Please.'

'Well, yeah, anyway, we got out at, like, Kensington High Street and Raf suddenly went under this, like, skyscraper and started looking up and shouting, "Colin, don't do it! It's not worth it!", then Zed joined in and these people started to crowd round to see what's going on – like, as if there's this bloke going to jump off the building or something.'

'What, in London? I didn't think they'd have cared.'

'No, there were, like, about twelve or twenty or something, all looking. And while me and Zed and Nic carried on shouting, Raf got his guitar out.'

'He had his guitar with him?'

'Yeah. I meant to say that. He'd just been to his lesson before we met him. So, anyway, he just starts, like, busking, playing this American Hi-Fi song, which I, like, hate, but it's okay 'cos it's so funny, and all these people suddenly start watching, and me and Zed and Nic are pissing ourselves laughing. But then Raf starts singing this other song, which is made up from the lyrics of this love letter we found.'

'So that story you started to tell first is really part of this story?'

'Yeah, I suppose. I shouldn't tell you what was in the letter, but it was so funny – all these really dorky lyrics about this girl's fluffy sweater and stuff. We kind of joined in on percussion and this woman – she was, like, really old, probably a librarian or something – said to Raf that he was going to be at the top of the charts one day.'

'Wow. But I guess Raf's not that bothered about being at the top of the charts, is he?'

'Not really. Well, maybe the metal charts.'

'And what happened next?'

'That was kind of it. All these people sort of walked away. It was so funny, though. I dunno. I suppose it was more of a visual thing.'

'No. It sounds like fun. I can't believe you got away with it. Did anyone ask you who Colin was?'

'No. They all realised we were joking pretty quickly. I suppose it was a bit of a crap story. Maybe I should have written it down, 'cos I missed a few parts out.'

'Maybe. It sometimes helps. What about the song that Raf made up? Is that in Goat Punishment's set now?'

'Yeah. Kind of. We called it "Soppy Geek (The Skyscraper Song)".'

'Talking Heads once made an album called *More Songs About Buildings And Food*. Maybe Goat Punishment could make one called *More Songs About Buildings And Geeks*.'

'Mmm. Er. Maybe. Who are Talking Heads?'

EDUCATING PETER — THE DEEP

If you're sentient and heading into Hull, it won't be long before you hear about The Deep. Most likely, you'll see it advertised on a car sticker, or you'll stop at a petrol station and a compassionate cashier, clocking that you're an out-of-towner, will nod knowingly at you and point you in its direction. If not, you're sure to be offered a flyer for it in a restaurant or shop, or spot one of its road signs, which, from the Humber Bridge onwards, seem to dominate every roundabout and junction, overshadowing other, less significant signposts such as 'City Centre', 'Railway Station' and 'Hospital'. Peter and I were pretty sure The Deep was something to do with fish, but beyond that we were more or less stumped.

'Perhaps it's the world's biggest fish and chip shop,' suggested Peter.

'I suppose people do eat a lot of fish and chips up here,' I agreed.

'Do you think that's a fish on the sign or a dolphin?' asked Peter.

'Perhaps it's a dolphin. Maybe we can go and see dolphins and throw balls at them and stuff.'

'No. Actually, that looks more like a fish, now I come to think of it.'

'Mmm. But if it's a fish and chip shop, why didn't they draw a chip on the sign as well?'

'Mmm. I dunno.'

'I suppose a chip's quite an ambiguous thing to draw. You could quite easily mistake it for, I dunno, a very small fencepost or something.'

'Or one of those very thin pencil erasers you sometimes get.'

'Hmm. Whatever it looked like, I'm sure it would taste better than Circulus's chips.'

'Yeah. Like, *way*.'

'Anyway, I think people up here are more into having gravy with their chips than fish.'

'But you couldn't really draw gravy, could you? What would that look like?'

'An amoeba?'

In the end, it took Jim Eldon to shed some light on the issue. 'The Deep?' chuckled Jim. 'I'll tell you what The Deep is. The Deep's a very good place for struggling musicians to make money. Everyone knows about The Deep around here. World's biggest submarium. A bit like an aquarium, but bigger.'

'And, er, sub-er?' I asked.

'Oh, very much so. I suggest you take a trip there later today. Well worth a visit while you're here.'

The Deep's queues were always long, but when they got even longer than normal, the management would sometimes ask Jim to play maritime songs to entertain the punters as they gazed out towards the murky North Sea. His knowledge of local folk music was gargantuan. But local folk music wasn't all that Jim played or studied, by a long, long way. Sometimes he'd adapt Elvis songs using just his violin. Other times he'd head down to a local pub with a group of friends and sit in a corner reinterpreting hard house and drum'n'bass – 'y'know, what d'ya call it, bangin' music?' – using the popular instruments of the nineteenth century. When it came to eclecticism, he made Beck seem about as adventurous as Status Quo.

I was somewhat ashamed, heading into our encounter, about how little research I'd done on Jim. My entire basis for meeting him boiled down to the tenuous fact that many years ago I'd heard him perform an amusing, fiddle-only version of Bruce Springsteen's air-punching rock anthem 'Dancing In The Dark' on Andy Kershaw's radio show. I knew next to nothing about his background, his dress sense, his personality, or the music he'd made in the intervening decade. Instinct and experience alone – the sort of instinct and experience that tells you that middle-aged men with fiddles tend to go hand-in-hand with good anecdotes – told me that he could provide a useful chapter of Peter's education, if not a hugely comfort-able one. Sometimes it seemed that, despite everything I'd taught him, Peter's musical parameters still stretched only as far as the space between AC/DC and Slipknot. I knew how he felt, of course: in my late teens, I'd possibly been even narrower. During the Eighties my dad had listened to Jim Eldon types – or

Croaky Weirdos, as I used to think of them – and I'd done my best to refuse to acknowledge their existence. Then, when I'd finally matured enough to appreciate them, it had been too late: my dad had moved on to something even less fashionable. I wasn't Peter's dad – scary, sometimes, how often I had to remind myself of this – but I could see him making the same mistake. I wasn't totally convinced it *was* a mistake – blocking too much out is, in a way, just as important a part of a music lover's evolution as letting too much in – but I wanted to get a better, closer insight into the workings of his teenage dogma, and by extension into the workings of *my* teenage dogma. Plonking him in a room together with Jim seemed like a good start.

Still, I had my misgivings about the experiment. Several weeks before, when I'd first spoken to him on the telephone, Jim had seemed jumpy and suspicious, and wanted reassurance that I didn't want a 'straight' interview. He spoke in a thick Yorkshire accent, paused for long periods, constructed verbal sentences more painstakingly than many people construct written ones, and explained he was worried about being 'represented' accurately, but calmed down slightly when I stressed the informal nature of the encounter and asked if he could play us some songs. He said he did a lot of work in schools, and seemed to like the idea, at least, of passing on his musical knowledge to a minor. But I detected an edginess in his voice and, as the Hull trip drew nearer, I began, once again, to fret on Peter's behalf. I'd arranged this leg of our adventure back in early spring, at a time when, having only met him once, I still knew him only as

Jenny's intractable son – another tiny piece of the irritating, amorphous adolescent mass that made my outdoor life a tiny bit less wholesome. Since then, though, something unforeseen had happened: I'd grown to enjoy his company. Much as it dented my pride to admit it, I no longer had the desire to put him in the middle of awkward, hard-boiled adult conversations that would test his fourteen-year-old attention span – no matter how interested I was in the results. Moreover, I was starting to have less interest in putting *me* in the middle of them.

Meeting Jim marked a veritable step backwards in my personal relationship with Peter, although not, I hoped, in our working one. With the exception of our conversation with Ed The Troubadour, he'd never been quieter, never shifted more in his chair, never moved his eyes more nervously from side to side. There were moments of hardship in every great apprenticeship – Luke Skywalker being forced to hang out in a swamp with an ancient shrivelled dwarf in *The Empire Strikes Back*, Buffy The Vampire Slayer having to spend excessive amounts of time pondering ancient texts in a musty library with a repressed bibliophile – and this was his. I only hoped that he saw it that way as well. He should have done, since he claimed to have watched *Star Wars* 104 times since receiving the video for his seventh birthday.

I'd described Jim Eldon to Peter as having a 'spiritual beard'. This was, in all honesty, pure guesswork. Face to face, he had more of a spiritual moustache. There was apparently nothing spiritual at all about the tattoos on his arms. Dressed in a

Hawaiian shirt and slacks as jet black as his hair, he looked younger than his age, which he couldn't remember exactly but knew was somewhere in the middle fifties. It was only when I looked more closely at his hair, his urgent watery eyes and the bric-a-brac in his house, that he began to remind me more of my grandparents' generation than my parents'.

With every road seemingly steering us back towards The Deep, it had taken us a while to find his house, a mid-twentieth-century terrace surrounded by several hundred other identical mid-twentieth-century terraces. Then, almost as soon as we'd arrived and been introduced to his wife, Lynette, the phone had started to ring. Evidently, it was an important call – a local promoter wondering, at length, if Jim would like to play second on the bill to punk stalwart Reckless Eric at the Hull Adelphi. I didn't mind; I was used to waiting around before interviews, but Peter was beginning to fiddle with his mobile phone. He might have had an unusual number of friends and an unusual number of computer gaming problems to solve, but today's level of text-messaging was more redolent of an international crisis than a slight hitch in the early stages of *Tomb Raider*. Unlike me, he couldn't even amuse himself by admiring Jim's John Barleycorn wall hangings or flicking through his Mike Waterson albums. If he'd tattooed the words 'What the hell am I doing here?' on his forehead, his thought process couldn't have been more blatant.

'Yeah,' Jim was saying into the mouthpiece. 'The thing is, you see, I'm working on boats at the moment, but there's some fellas on there I'd love to get together.

This bloke Diggy. Sometimes he'll just start to sing. This is what I'm trying to express to you.'

It was a relief to hear that Jim sounded just as apprehensive and convoluted talking to other people on the phone as he did talking to me. It was also a relief to hear he had friends called 'Diggy'. Every minute or two, he'd mention his work on 'boats'. What exactly did this entail? Was Jim a shipmate? A caterer? A fisherman? It occurred to me that he probably didn't make a living exclusively from his songs, which he released autonomously via mail order. It also occurred to me that not many people making honest, organic music in the British Isles did any more. It was a depressing concept and I hoped that, somewhere between text messages, Peter was going to take it on board.

In reality, this was a fruitful period for Jim. His boat work, he explained when he came off the phone, involved entertaining the passengers of the *Yorkshire Bell*, a cruise ship that went back and forth between Hull and Whitby. He'd mix local, traditional numbers, like 'Dogger Bank' and 'Oh What A Windy Night', with universal favourites like 'My Grandfather's Clock', along with the odd rock and roll classic. From the way he told it, he'd just get right up in the passengers' faces, without any announcement. To demonstrate, he picked up his fiddle from the corner of the room and launched into a minimalist rendition of 'Wooden Heart', a folk song made famous by Elvis. Out of the corner of my eye, I saw Peter flinch slightly, in the way that you might if you stumbled across someone a couple of generations above you getting naked.

'I think music embarrasses people,' said Jim, laying his fiddle aside. 'I mean, look, you were embarrassed there. There's not necessarily anything wrong with it.'

Peter flinched again.

'I think you're right,' I said. 'I was embarrassed. But I still want you to play me another song.'

Jim didn't like to sum up his music, and had more trouble doing so than anyone I'd ever met. His sentences would usually begin with the phrase 'The thing is,' then express very simple things in a needlessly complicated, stumbling manner; things that, when boiled down to their true essence, probably amounted to the folk equivalent of an indie bonus. What Jim seemed reluctant to express were opinions – about the state of folk music, about the youth of today, about Hull, about why the folk community went for his interpretation of 'Dancing In The Dark' in such a big way. It left me, as the instigator of this bizarre get-together, facing a dilemma: encourage more conversation and make Jim feel uncomfortable, or encourage more fiddle-playing and make Peter feel uncomfortable.

Where Ed The Troubadour had been outspoken, Jim was introverted, yet there was nothing unemotional or offhand about him. He looked you square in the eye when he spoke or sang, and, despite all his fuzzy prevaricating, I got the impression he was trying to answer my questions honestly. His advice to Peter was too tangled to relate in full here, but was undoubtedly sincere, and seemed to contain an intrinsically solid message about penetrating the bullshit topping of modern music to its emotional core. At one point, during a story about an elderly Italian lady on the *Yorkshire Bell* who'd described one of his songs as 'like a tarantella', tears filled his eyes and he left the room for thirty seconds, announcing, 'I'm sorry . . . This means so much to me. I think I'm going to blub.' It was hard not to be overwhelmed by the pathos, and for the first time all afternoon, Peter laid his mobile phone to one side, mid-text message.

Later, after much hesitation, Jim showed us the words to 'I'm Agency', a song he'd written about the myriad temping jobs he'd endured. The song was essentially just a list, containing everything from fruit-picking to toilet-cleaning – very much, I noted proudly, in the vein of 'Rick Argues' by Rick Argues. But in the end, this gesture probably said more than anything about Jim. In more than half a decade of turning up at strangers' houses and asking them about their musical lives, several taboos had been snapped: I'd been shown underwear, sex toys and kinky footwear. But I'd never once been exposed to a lyric book.

The problem with Jim, from Peter's point of view, wasn't that he wasn't a nice bloke. He was. The problem wasn't that he didn't have a sense of humour. Anyone who tried to reinterpret 'bangin'' drum'n'bass with a fiddle had to have some sense of the ridiculous. The problem was that when you got close to his life, there was a very adult intensity to it – an intensity speckled with humour, certainly, but a very intense, complex humour that a teenage brain might refuse to administer. Peter had described Ed The Troubadour to his mates as 'the Hobbit bloke with the axe', but it was doubtful Jim could be reduced to such a simple soundbite, and 'the bloke with the dyed hair, the loud shirt, the air of hardship and the strangely hesitant and stiff way of speaking' didn't have the same ring to it. 'During adolescence, children are starting to think for themselves and make their own judgements,' I'd read the previous night in *Adolescence: The Survival Guide*. I got the feeling, however, that Peter wouldn't make a judgement about Jim at all; he'd simply block the whole experience out – even the sparse, juddering rendition of 'Jailhouse Rock' that Jim had performed to herald our departure. Later, though – maybe many, many years later – he'd remember it. Already, a back engine room of his brain had probably fed it into its hard drive. It was, after all, a unique experience. I certainly wasn't going to forget it in a hurry, and, as I headed back towards The Deep, I attempted to sort my emotions into some semblance of order:

1. Guilt, for asking Jim too much.
2. More guilt, for exposing Peter to too much.
3. Elation, at having fulfilled my ambition to get lost on a council estate in Hull.
4. Gratification, at having experienced a private musical performance of a downright unusual and precious nature.
5. Impatience, at not having been to The Deep yet.
6. Desire, to buy Peter a packet of crisps.

Crisps weren't The Deep's strong point, but it did sell a heck of a lot of cod. On the radio, everyone was talking about it. Well, not everyone: Steve Wright, on Radio Two, was following an ironic aside about the dress sense of someone who used to be in Sad Café with an even more ironic aside about the facial hair of someone who used to be in Foreigner, while John Humphries, on Radio Four, was rudely interrupting a politician. But in and around Hull, the big topic was cod, and whether the world's biggest submarium had the right to sell it in its restaurant when it was virtually an endangered species. Kevin from North Hull felt that it was 'a bit weird admiring fish, then eating them in the same place', but Linda from Grimsby was more philosophical, suggesting, 'It's not a proper fish, is it? Not like them pretty ones.' I had to say, overall, I was with Kevin on this one.

To be fair, Peter and I didn't see any live cod at The Deep. We did, however, see a hammerhead shark that looked like former England striker Alan Shearer. The Deep might have thrived in the middle of the day, but forty minutes before closing time it was a ghost town, strewn with empty Solero wrappers and tired-looking computer screens that were supposed to tell you the origins of the sea but didn't. At one point we were excited to see a small pool advertising fish you could touch. At another point, two seconds later, we were slightly less excited to see a sign below it announcing that the touching fish were 'tired' and had been given an 'early bedtime'. How exactly did you make a fish 'tired'? I wondered, my head filling with images of aquatic badminton, inter-tank volleyball and games of fetch involving driftwood and particularly obedient koi carp. More to the point, how did you give it an early bedtime? Did you read to it for twenty minutes and hope it nodded off under one of those ornamental underwater caves? You had to hand it to The Deep: it was deep. It also had some great features. Today, though, something monumental had passed through it – if not a shoal of rioting cod, then at least a party of very unruly schoolchildren – and left its mark.

'It's like a town in one of those old Westerns, just after Clint Eastwood or someone has gone through it,' observed Peter. 'Except with fish.'

Once again, I was enjoying talking to Peter about random rubbish surrounding music (or fish, in this case) more than I was enjoying talking to him about music itself. It was slightly alarming how quickly our pupil–teacher relationship had accelerated, with rock and roll becoming just another academic subject, albeit one taught slightly more haphazardly. Sometimes, when I related a well-known anecdote about a television going through a hotel room window or a heavy metal hellraiser defiling a national monument, it could feel worrying, like I was talking about Third World debt or the ins and outs of the private sector. It didn't matter that what I was lecturing about was wild and rebellious; what mattered – and what was responsible for the occasional absent look in Peter's eyes – was that I was an older person setting the agenda, trying to make too much sense of the world on Peter's behalf. I tried to stay conscious of keeping a fun, freewheeling element to proceedings, of encouraging Peter to learn in the direction that he wanted to learn, just like the teachers at his strangely laid-back school did. Whatever Peter had thought about today's meeting with Jim, though, I could be pretty sure he hadn't seen it as anything to do with

flexible learning. Whatever hidden riches the experience had held, you couldn't say it had a lot of *bend*. I'd
hoped that forcing Peter to interact with Jim would
give me an insight into Peter's thinking, but now it was
over, his brain remained a mystery, and one that
was just a little further from my grasp than it had been
a couple of weeks before.

Now I wanted to atone for our misadventure with an
activity that was impulsive and loose. The only
problem was, we were on the Yorkshire–Lincolnshire
border, a place more renowned for its high rate of road
casualties than its musical legends and landmarks. I
quickly ransacked my brain, but could only really
come up with Mick Ronson, David Bowie's old
guitarist, who was dead. There was always the
Beautiful South, but I had a dim recollection that their
lead singer was busy working in a petrol station in a
TV soap opera. I also had a less dim recollection that I
didn't care. In desperation, I turned on the radio and
manual-tuned to 828 medium wave, the frequency
that (usually) played host to my favourite European
radio station, AERO CLASSICROCK. Immediately, I
felt calmer.

Being able to tune in to AERO CLASSICROCK is, to
me, one of the chief joys of living near one of the outer
points of the East Coast of England. For those un-
familiar with it, AERO CLASSICROCK is a Dutch
station whose name tells you everything you need to
know about its modus operandi: wall-to-wall, in your
face, unashamedly fashion-free rock music around the
clock. Since AERO CLASSICROCK isn't even
supposed to be broadcast in the British Isles, I've never

seen it advertised or listed, yet you can just tell that its name is capitalised, in the same way that you can just tell that the man who does the horror movie trailer voiceovers at the cinema is over six feet tall and owns a drinks cabinet. AERO CLASSICROCK doesn't have disc jockeys, just occasional goofy between-song voices that say things like, 'LUNCHBOX!', 'ROAD-RUNNER!' and 'ROCK OF AGES!' for no sensible reason. In fact, it's quite feasible that AERO CLASSICROCK is not a radio station at all, just one big randomly shuffled mix tape, yet somehow this matters not a jot. For any man honest enough to get in touch with his inner Homer Simpson, the station remains a full-throttle, life-affirming experience. The fact that it can descend into painful sizzling noises in bad weather and that on a Saturday afternoon, in the ten-mile area directly north of my house, it mysteriously shares half its bandwidth with a farming programme just makes it all the more special.

Now, listening to U2's 'Sunday Bloody Sunday' back-to-back with Todd Rundgren's 'I Saw The Light' back-to-back with Styx's 'Renegade', I marvelled at my stupidity. Over the past few weeks I'd laboured over such home-mix tapes as 'Mystic Britain, 1968–73', 'Fuzz Pedal Guerillas, 1971–75' and 'Families With Beards, August 1972–June 1973', trying to tailor my pupil's musical exposure to perfection, when the answer was right in front of me all along. Here, in hissy yet vital form, was everything you could ever want to know about real, good-time music – the kind that transcends fashion and adolescence and, well, everything, apart from life itself. Here were

Foreigner, singing about how the woman in their woman brought out the man in their man. Here were The Faces, smelling of booze, fags and neglected hair on 'Stay With Me', building, building, building to the show-off guitar hook of the century, then talking sexist crap, but doing it brilliantly. Here was Rod Stewart in his prime: a black 1930s blues singer disguised as a vertically challenged scarecrow posing as the ultimate sex slob. This was Man's Music, and we were both Men – or at least we both soon would be – in the middle of a Man's Trip, and this was what we needed to make us both believe in it, to make it stop feeling like work. If I'd been stopped at a traffic light, I would probably have run off into nearby woodland. *This* was the essence! Sod 'ammunition'. *This* was what Peter had to get in touch with at any cost! Isn't this just the most awesome thing? I thought.

'Isn't this just the most awesome thing?' I asked Peter.

But he was asleep.

PENTANGLE – BASKET OF LIGHT
(TRANSATLANTIC, 1970)

Tom: 'The early Seventies was a time of musical symbiosis, with black and white, folk and rock, soul and country, funk and blues feeding off one another like never before and never since. Pentangle were the quintessential folk band for the time, catching the tail end of the psychedelic movement and mixing a spiritual Led Zeppelin-type aura with a knack for very traditional, very English melody.

'*Basket Of Light* is their most bewitching album, largely because of the production, which conjures up the image of a group of hirsute angels composing hymns to the starving earth in an enormous wooden auditorium with moss on its eaves. Here, the group mix traditional tunes with original ones, and it's hard to tell one from the other. Songs like "I Once Had A Sweetheart" and "Springtime Promises" are richer than the parallel work of Fairport Convention, more attuned to the land than the equivalent warblings of Mellow Candle. Vocalist Jacqui McShee is a seraph in clogs, and if Bert Jansch's co-vocals are occasionally weedy, it's less in an effete way and more in a way redolent of the things that grow in the ground. Normally, you'd have to roll around in the mud beneath an agricultural museum for weeks to make a record this at one with the great old outdoors; Pentangle, apparently, did it in a recording studio. Their songs are tinted with acid, but, as with all the best folk, ultimately you get the sense that they could have been written and recorded at any point during the last thousand years.'

Peter: 'I'm sorry. This annoys the piss out of me.'

EDUCATING PETER

THE BIG SLEEP

It's hard to pinpoint the exact moment that I decided youth culture was dead. Looking back, I could possibly narrow it down to the moment I initially became aware of The Stereophonics, or a day in 1994 when I first saw a bootleg screen print of Kurt Cobain with a shotgun in his mouth, or the first time I felt the urge to strangle a skate kid. Or perhaps, on a more general level, I could posthumously attach some sort of ominous significance to Blur beating Oasis to number one in the singles chart in the summer of 1995. But that would probably be a little too neat. Much as I'd like to think there was a pivotal event that gave definition to my change of heart, it's far more likely that comprehension crept up on me gradually, until finally the all-consuming young person's pursuit of Keeping Up felt hollow and pointless.

Of course, there was the possibility that youth culture hadn't gone off at all; that it was me who was stale. But, in the end, that was immaterial. The important thing was that *my* youth culture was dead: the bands that I had loved as a teenager had either disintegrated or gone out of fashion, the clothes that I'd worn had vanished from the high street, the arthouse movie icons I'd worshipped had gone bald or blockbuster, and the mutual beliefs that had helped hold my network of friends together had fragmented into something more complex. If these intrinsic elements of coming-of-age had been replaced by others that seemed just as important to the generation that followed me, then I wasn't going to waste my time trying to understand why. Attempting to comprehend why anyone would want to listen to Papa Roach or watch *Dawson's Creek* seemed far too difficult a proposition. It was far easier – and a lot more fun – to take the view that youth culture had been hijacked and transformed into something meaningless and corporate.

The question that interested me was: would Peter feel the same in thirteen years' time? It was hard to imagine that something even more meaningless and quasi-alternative than Slipknot would arrive a few years from now, hoodwink a new generation and leave my fresh-faced companion feeling as world-weary as I felt. But fifty years of pop culture evolution told me it was perfectly possible. And the more time I spent with Peter, the more I understood why.

Spending time with Peter didn't change the way I felt about youth culture; it just changed the way I thought about it. Three months into our curriculum, I still let out an involuntary Sideshow Bob shiver in the vicinity of Puddle Of Mudd albums, couldn't understand why anyone would want to give Heath Ledger a starring role in a movie, and had absolutely no desire to attach a long, purposeless piece of metal to my trousers. Yet, at the same time, I clocked a flaw in my gloomy philosophising. In believing that youth culture was sour and jaded, I'd made the mistake of believing that the people who consumed it were sour and jaded as well. I'd forgotten that, due to their singular lack of perspective, teenagers would always be teenagers. *They* didn't know that the generations preceding them had reserved all the good clothes and tunes, and even if they did, why should they care? They had other, more important matters to worry about, like finding an effective brand of spot-remover or getting Denise Jones in 8D to notice them in the quadrangle at breaktime.

When Peter flabbergasted me, he tended to flabbergast me because of his sheer teenageness – a kind of awkward adolescent essence that, in the aftermath of the American teen flick revolution and Harry Enfield's Kevin The Teenager sketches, seemed almost too clichéd to be true. Sometimes, when he hunched his shoulders or buried his hands in his sleeves or overslept in a comic fashion or grunted unintelligibly or repeated a catchphrase from *Buffy The Vampire Slayer*, I'd assume he was making some kind of postmodern statement. I'd forget, for a moment, that he wasn't one of my own twenty-something mates, mimicking one of the classic teen qualities for effect. Then it would hit me that he was just being a typical fourteen-year-old; that to him, these actions weren't yet clichés, and that, even if they were, clichés had a slightly different meaning when your chief priority in life was gaining acceptance. Then I'd take some time to ponder this, momentarily awestruck by this weird state halfway between childhood and adulthood that I, bafflingly, had also occupied not too long ago.

Oversleeping, in particular, was almost a point of adolescent pride for Peter. He talked about getting up in time for the Sunday *EastEnders* omnibus with the same fervour that I talked about getting up in time to hear the dawn chorus. The logistic preamble to our trips had a pattern to them: I'd initially speak to Jenny and make an arrangement, then, later, speak to Peter, who would adjust our meeting time by a couple of hours, claiming that this mum had forgotten that he had 'coursework' to do in the morning. I found it strange that Peter, who was yet to begin his GCSEs, would have coursework, and even stranger that someone with so much energy who didn't work for a living would want to waste so much of the day in bed. I also wondered exactly who was in charge here. As the teacher, wasn't I the one who was supposed to set the starting time for the lesson?

I'd known for a while that it was only a matter of time before Peter's lethargy ate into our schedule to detrimental effect, so, as I stood outside Sloane Square tube station, peering anxiously towards the exit gate, I couldn't say I was surprised. Thirteen times in half an hour I'd looked up the number listed under 'Thardoz' in my mobile phone's address book. Thirteen times in half an hour I'd scolded myself for not buying a phone with a redial button on it. Thirteen times in half an hour I'd been met with Peter's singularly unmoved answerphone message: 'Er. Yeah. This is Pete. Now *you* say something . . .'. Perhaps he was stuck in a tube tunnel with no reception, but instinct told me otherwise. If I was being totally honest with myself, I'd seen this coming the previous evening, when Jenny had called to inform me that Peter would be spending the night at Zed's house and making his own way to our rendezvous point. I had, after all, witnessed Peter in inaction in the morning and, helpful as I'm sure Zed's parents were, I couldn't imagine them coaxing him into his start-the-day bath with quite the same zeal as Jenny. Not, that is, unless they owned a particularly high-powered set of electric cattle prods.

I looked at my watch. Then, remembering I didn't have a watch, I looked at my mobile phone. In minus five minutes, Peter and I were scheduled to meet Jenny Fabian, one of the world's most famous former rock and roll groupies, next to the July issue of *Golf World* in the Sloane Square branch of W. H. Smith's. I gave Peter's number one last try then finally moved away, immediately going to work on excuses for my charge's absence.

Fabian represented something of a last-minute addition to Peter's curriculum. It had struck me, as I'd reached the halfway stage in my adventures with him, that his education was somewhat lacking in female perspective. In order to rectify this, I'd immediately made an attempt to contact some of the hippest, best-known female stars in the music industry. Then, when their agents had asked me to put my request in writing and thrown my fax in the bin without looking at it, I'd attempted to contact some of the least hip, lesser-known ones. These included Stacia, the buxom nude dancer from prog rockers Hawkwind, Stevie Langer, the woman with the big voice who'd sung the theme tune for the Bodyform sanitary towels advert, and Fabian.

Langer had either failed to get or decided to ignore the message I'd left at the music shop she was affiliated to, and Stacia, from what I could ascertain from the many sci-fi-obsessed fansites devoted to pictures of her breasts, had married a blues musician and relocated to Germany, but Fabian had returned my call within the space of an hour. She spoke a saucy hippy version of the Queen's English, made tongue-in-cheek references to 'getting the old fishnets out', and remained in good humour when, while I was describing the thesis for my project, she fell under the misapprehension that I had described her as 'a British rock landmark'. I was impressed, and more impressed still when she actually seemed *more* keen to partake in an interview *because* I had a teenager in tow.

But now he wasn't here.

A fortnight earlier, with Peter's mum's approval, I'd passed my copy of Fabian's autobiographical 1969 novel, *Groupie*, on to Peter in order to prepare for today, and I was starting to think that maybe this hadn't been such a smart move. The book, which tells the tale of a well-heeled nineteen-year-old who shags her way through Swinging Sixties London, is full of references to 'plating', 'getting high', 'kinky sex' and a myriad other activities a fourteen-year-old probably wouldn't dream of imagining people older than his parents indulging in. Sure, *I* might have been able to get past the fact that the book had been written thirty-odd years ago and that its creator was now old enough to relate to an episode of *Last Of The Summer Wine*, but in Peter's mind it probably fell under the catch-lots category of Strange Old People's Stuff That It's Best Not To Know About. It was quite probable that he saw the prospect of meeting Fabian in the same way that the sixteen-year-old me had seen the prospect of having my cheeks pinched by Doris, the over-affectionate, overperfumed, middle-aged checkout supervisor at the Tesco supermarket where I once worked. In truth, I imagined Peter had read the first few pages of *Groupie*, got to the bit where Katie, the heroine, plates the lead singer of the Satin Odyssey, cast it onto the same pile that he'd cast most of the other texts I'd given him, and turned his attention back to mastering the riff to 'Enter Sandman'. And, to be honest, I couldn't blame him.

As it turned out, though, he had little reason to be frightened.

Over the years, I'd got used to interviewing people who didn't look much like my mental image of them, but in the flesh Jenny Fabian looked so little like my impression of Katie that, upon shaking her hand, it was impossible to conceal my double-take. A frighteningly petite woman with a pink streak in her grey hair and the legwear of an early Nineties grunge fan, she resembled the world's coolest grandma, but certainly not the obvious grown-up incarnation of the spirit of headstrong Sixties free-living. Strolling along the King's Road next to her, I couldn't help feeling like some form of lumbering security guard, employed to protect something brittle.

It was embarrassing, after Fabian had been agreeable enough to meet me, having to explain to her that the whole reason for this encounter was probably at this moment asleep on someone's kitchen floor using a can of Silly String as a pillow, but she took the news well. For the following two hours, the two of us walked the length of the King's Road, stopping as Fabian pointed out her old hang-outs – bohemian coffee houses, hairdressers that specialised in giving you 'the Brian Jones' regardless of your sex, and boutiques, most of which had now been replaced by travel agents or branches of Pizza Express. The world of *Groupie* – a plethora of chicks, pads and casual plating – was gone almost without a trace, and as she indulged me in a game of Name The Inspiration, it transpired that many of the thinly disguised real-life stars of the book were now dead (one of the few who wasn't was Syd Barrett, another of Fabian's sexual conquests). I'd assumed that revisiting her old haunts was something Fabian was used to, but, as we stood outside the house she used to share with the whiney psychedelic rock band Family, she revealed that she hadn't actually been back here since the late Sixties. For the first time, she seemed emotional about her past, and for the first time, I really, really wished Peter was here, too. Later, she took me to a shoe shop and let me help her pick out a pair of bright orange slip-ons, and I wished Peter was here considerably less.

In the Seventies, Fabian had forsaken the rock and roll life to hang out in the country with equestrian types with 'Sir' before their name. These days, she was dabbling in music journalism and coming towards the completion of a sequel to *Groupie* with her co-writer Johnny Byrne, but she talked more like an unusually clued-up member of rural high society than a washed-up hepcat, enthusing about hare-coursing, and recalling classic psychedelic bands in the same way that pundits on retro TV programmes recall slightly kitsch toys that they've grown out of.

Before meeting her, I'd been unsure of the kind of lesson she could offer Peter, but now I understood – sort of. As an example of rock and roll moving towards the end of middle-age, Fabian was a great illustration of how, today, the Sixties seemed so far away yet simultaneously so close – a living lesson in the passage of time in a musical world and its attendant pathos. At one point in the none-too-distant past she'd needed all the proximity to fame and talent and hip, happening things she could get – not to mention the concomitant plating – to feel fulfilled. Now she bought a pair of garish shoes and went home happy. At one point her generation had wanted to change the world with peace and love. Now they were deliberately nasty to small furry animals and didn't feel bad about it. It got me thinking about how the moral and artistic values that I'd held onto as if my life depended upon them ten years ago already seemed silly, and would soon probably seem even sillier, and about how the same thing would happen to Peter before too long, whether he liked it or not. The whole thing gave you a unique sense of perspective. Well, it gave me a unique sense of perspective, anyway. I had my doubts as to whether Peter would have been willing to stop thinking about computer games, crisps and

Swugelbacker Airbuses for long enough to dwell on it. And besides, wasn't ignoring what adults told you about how you wouldn't be young for very long the whole point of *being* young?

About an hour after I'd met up with Fabian, I finally received a call from Peter, who was still at Zed's house and claimed that he'd run out of credit on his mobile phone and forgotten what tube station we were supposed to meet at, yet failed to explain why this had prevented him from calling me from a landline ninety minutes earlier. At this point I made it quite clear to him that, if he was going to at least say hello to Fabian, he had to hotfoot it over to Chelsea from North London in under an hour. True to my expectations, he turned up sixty-three minutes later, lolloping (less true to my expectations) cheerfully into the King's Road branch of Waterstones in a manner more redolent of a fan of *Herbie Goes Bananas* than *The Crow*.

'You're too late,' I told him. 'She left about two minutes ago.'

'Oh, bummer. Soz. But this thing's shit.' He dangled his miniature phone scornfully between his thumb and forefinger. 'Was she pissed off?'

'Not really. She's really quite—'

'Cool. That's a relief. Hey, guess what? It was dead funny. There was this kid at this party last night, Nigel. We call him Nozzle Man, 'cos he's got this weird nose. Anyway, you should meet him, he's dead cool, he likes a lot of the music you like – Aerosmith, you like them, don't you? Well, he lent me this tape – and his dad's like this film director or something. Well, like films for TV. But yeah . . . His dad's got this garage full of space hoppers. They're these Seventies inflatable things with ears that you hold on to. I guess you remember them, but I hadn't heard of them and they are sooo cool. There were about nine in all, and me, Raf and Nozzle Man and a couple of other kids just started bouncing down his road on them. It's a cul-de-sac so there are no cars really. It was so, so cool – there were all these grannies looking out of windows and stuff. Then we went in and had this game of Rude Scrabble and I had the top, like, word score thingy – a triple, with 'Bumcake'. You know, from that song in *This Is Spinal Tap*? I know it's not a word and stuff, but that was kind of okay . . . I can't even remember what time I went to sleep.'

He paused at last to catch his breath.

'So you had a good time then?' I asked him.

'No. Yeah. The best. Like, dead funny.'

'And you got around to watching *This Is Spinal Tap*? I'm impressed . . .'

'*Yeah!* I've seen it six times now. Well, six and a half, really.'

'What about *Groupie*? Did you get chance to have a look at that?'

'Oh, no, shit. I forgot.'

It was nice to see Peter so upbeat, and I felt a dilemma approaching. On the one hand, I felt slightly hurt about how little he seemed to care that he'd let me down, and felt that some sort of penance was in order from him. On the other, it was gratifying to hear him talking so enthusiastically and embracing the universe above shoe level, and I sensed that I should be taking advantage of this.

I'd seen Peter in a post-party state before, but today was different. The signs were immediately familiar to me: the sunken yet euphoric eyes . . . the delayed reaction times . . . the uninhibited anecdotes . . . the lazy smile that seemed to look at the world from a slight angle and find it a thing of unlimited surreal wonder . . . the slightly stale aroma wafting up from his leather jacket. I was suddenly glad that Peter hadn't met Jenny Fabian – and not just because of the odour of his jacket. The last thing he needed right now was a yawn-inducing lesson from me about the transience of youth. He was too busy experiencing his own epiphany, and I was too busy feeling grateful to be caught in the middle of it to deny him.

Last night, I realised, Peter had been drunk for the first time.

Not wildly drunk, maybe. Probably not even drunk enough to lose his inhibitions. But drunk enough to feel better about himself and to never think alcohol tasted horrible again, or at least not to let that be a factor in stopping him consuming it.

As the most tenuous, unrelated of guardian figures, I had a uniquely divided perspective on this revelation. One portion of me worried on behalf of Jenny. Another felt morally outraged that teenagers seemed to be drinking at younger and younger ages these days. Another told that part to shut up, be realistic, and remember the night in 1989 when me and Matthew Read had downed five cans of Special Brew each and walked up the street adjacent to our secondary school, twanging car wing mirrors. Another part forgot that Peter was fourteen at all and felt the urge to pat him on the back and treat him to a pint of the hair of the dog that bit him. Another part felt a little like Janet, the fifty-year-old subject of a case study from *Adolescence: The Survival Guide*.

'We were delighted that he suddenly wanted to talk to us again,' Janet had explained about her teenage son, Chris. 'We would have long conversations about his friends, his problems, the state of the world, the existence of God. The only thing was he wanted to wake us up and have these talks sitting on the end of our bed at one in the morning when he'd just got home from an evening out with his friends.'

I could see Janet's point: it *was* irritating how teenagers only seemed to want to open up to you when you were most irritated with them. But, ultimately, I had it easy. Peter hadn't woken me up. Neither, mercifully, had he tried to get me into a conversation about the existence of God or shown me any of his poetry. It wasn't my responsibility to show him why drinking was wrong, and when and where he could and couldn't be overenthusiastic about life. I was, I had to remind myself, teaching him to *embrace* rock and roll, not to run and hide from it. Besides, alcohol seemed to be having an entirely positive effect on him, if you ignored the smell of his jacket: during the hour that I walked along the King's Road with him, retracing the steps I'd taken with Jenny Fabian, pointing out where record shops, cafés, bookshops and boutiques with names like Middle Earth and Granny Takes A Trip used to be, I didn't once lose him to a silent, melancholic reverie or hear him use the word 'nnghhh' as a form of communication.

No: moral outrage and responsibility be damned. Peter seemed to be seeing unusually clearly and it was my job, as his teacher, to make the most of this by putting the correct objects in his immediate vision. For the moment, I wasn't going to question him about last night's experience; I wasn't even going to comment on it. I was going to ride on the crest of my gothic friend's receptive post-booze rapture and use it in a manner that served both myself and our adventure in the most convenient manner possible. And I was going to start by asking him a question that I'd been meaning to ask him for several weeks – a difficult question that would always be harsh to spring upon any innocent human being, but, nevertheless, a question that I felt, now more than ever, to be a crucial element to our studies.

'Do you fancy going to Nottingham?'

PAPER v. STONE: THE SHOWDOWN

'So, where is it, like, exactly? I've never really been there. My mum has. I know it's somewhere up north, but not that far north, and I know they said it was the most violent city in England, after London.'

'You mean you really don't know? How can you know what the capital of Kenya is but not know where Nottingham is? I didn't know where Nairobi was when I was your age, but I knew where Milton Keynes was.'

'But that's different.'

'Why?'

'Well, you grew up in the Eighties. And you were in Nottingham.'

'So?'

'So they probably didn't teach you stuff like that, I guess.'

'But you said you didn't know where Nottingham was. So how can you know what kind of stuff they didn't teach me when I lived there?'

'I dunno.'

'Anyway, don't worry about it. It's sandwiched between Leicester and Sheffield.'

'I *think* I know where they are.'

'I don't believe it.'

'What?'

'Nothing.'

'Anyway, why are we going there?'

'It's a surprise.'

'It's not another groupie, is it?'

'No.'

'What's plating?'

'Ha! So you did read the book!'

'I dunno. I kind of, like, looked at it . . . but not much.'

'Ha! Your teachers were right – you are an enigma . . . Plating's what hippies called giving someone a blow job.'

'No way!'

'Way.'

'Gross!'

'Yeah.'

'Ugh.'

'This traffic's really pissing me off.'

'Mmmm.'

'Do you want me to put something else on the stereo? I expect you've had enough of *The Best Of Wings* now, haven't you? Put one of yours on if you want.'

'I dunno. I'm a bit bored with most of that stuff.'

'Do you want to play Stone, Paper, Scissors?'

'Alright. Ha. Wicked. I won. Paper wraps rock.'

'I never understood that. What damage exactly is

Paper doing to Stone by wrapping it? Surely a stone can't suffocate.'

'Hmmngh. When Raf and me play it we have another thing. As well as Stone, Scissors and Paper, we have Telephone Box. That traps everything inside it, except Stone, which can break its windows.'

'But how do you imitate a telephone box with one hand?'

'Like this.'

'Mmm. Impressive.'

'There's Sparrow as well, which pecks Paper to death, but gets its beak blunted by Stone.'

'And who wins out of Sparrow and Telephone Box?'

'Sparrow. It builds a nest in the handset.'

'Ooh. Painful. Do you and Raf ever feel like you have too much free time on your hands?'

'Sometimes.'

'So what made you change your mind?'

'What do you mean?'

'About drinking.'

'Oh . . . Er. Well, it was just like, I dunno, after I'd had more than one can it just tasted better. And stuff just kind of seemed . . . I dunno, funnier? It's just like the space hoppers. Normally that would have been funny, but last night it really made us piss ourselves. And this morning I woke up and Raf had put this can of Silly String under my head as a pillow and it was . . . I dunno. Just ace. I don't think I'd do it, though – y'know, like really getting drunk – unless I was with my mates.'

'But you're with your mates a lot, aren't you?'

'Hmmgh. I suppose.'

EDUCATING PETER

REALLY LOW-FI

I'd initially wanted to take Peter to Nottingham because I felt it was important, at this stage in our studies, to show him that not too long ago I, too, was a music-mad teenager, striving for direction, meaning and the most obscene t-shirt logos known to man. Taking him on a guided tour of my own personal musical evolution, I sensed, could only give him a greater understanding of my teachings and a greater respect for my wisdom. Here, among the endlessly sprouting *Big Issue* salespeople and theme pubs of my hometown, he would be reassured to find the landmarks of a time when I was just like him, only with even less symmetrical hair. Then, I hoped, he would put two scruffy, moody teenagers together, notice the similarities, and come up with the natural assumption that, from this point on, everything I said about rock and roll, food, the opposite sex, alcohol, crisps and life itself could only be the gospel truth.

That was my main reason for taking him to Nottingham, anyway.

There was one additional incentive.

A few weeks previously, I'd read a report in a broadsheet newspaper about the worryingly 'teenage' qualities of the current generation of twenty-somethings: my generation. According to the report's conclusions, people in their twenties were finding it increasingly hard to shake off the tastes and habits of their late childhood and were shirking responsibilities that previous generations had considered an obligation – responsibilities such as marriage, house buying, home cooking, remaining financially independent and refraining from listening to sadistic dance music at unsociable volumes.

As a married twenty-seven-year-old who hadn't prevailed upon his family for monetary support in more than a decade, and whose principal form of socialising revolved around the local golf club, I couldn't help feeling a little put out by this, not to mention somewhat jealous. It wasn't fair: even after hanging out with one of the teenage ranks for the best part of a summer, *I* didn't feel like an adolescent. I couldn't remember the last time I'd been bored, never mind the last time I'd been bored enough to listen to sadistic dance music at unsociable volumes. Yet, as this report would have it, I was the exception to the rule, and in spite of my best intentions I began to show signs of envy and mistrust. Could it be possible, I wondered, that my friends weren't telling me something – that they didn't *really* spend their free time filling out direct debit forms and striving to track down reliable plumbers, and that instead, behind my back, they hung out in packs around the entrance of Kentucky Fried Chicken, smoking and giving one another wedgies?

'What are you up to tonight?' I asked Steve and Sue Golden, a couple of days after reading the report.

'You know,' said Sue, 'winding down. Doing a bit of cooking. Making the weekly phone call to our parents. Steve wants to go to Pets At Home to get Molly a cat hammock, but I'm a bit too tired.'

'What about after that?' I persevered.

'Well,' said Steve, 'they're repeating *Nigella Bites* on UK Food. I was thinking I might watch that.'

'And after that?'

'Er, going to bed, I guess.'

'Hmm,' I mused, not totally convinced. 'It's just . . . I heard there was a good nu-metal night going on in Croydon these days. Two pounds a pint all night.'

'What the fuck are you on about?'

Even my wife could not be held above suspicion.

'What's that?' I asked her in the wake of a shopping trip to Norwich city centre, eyeing the somewhat familiar long metallic strip protruding from her Top Shop bag.

'It's a belt. Why?' said Edie.

'And where will you be putting this belt?'

'Around the top of my trousers, like most belts.'

'So it won't be dangling uselessly down your leg?'

'No. What are you talking about?'

'Nothing. Just checking.'

'You're weird.'

Clearly, I was being somewhat paranoid. I remained on guard, though. Okay, so I felt pretty sure that my best friends weren't attending The *Smash Hits* Awards party behind my back, but that wasn't to say that they weren't whispering about me in an equally treacherous manner for being unusually old and boring for my age. The more I thought about it, the more it began to sound worryingly true. The unswerving penchant for the music of my parents' generation, the golf, the fuzzy dressing gowns, the bowel-emulsifying aversion to nightclubs – perhaps, by normal standards, I *was* freakishly unteenage. I shuddered. Perhaps everyone who knew me thought this about me. Automatically my mind zipped back, microfiche-style, to a moment in 1991 when my golf mate – *my golf mate* – Ashley Bates had called me a 'grandad' for not dancing to The Shamen's indie dance hit 'Move Any Mountain'. Perhaps everyone who knew me had *always* thought this about me – even when I was a teenager.

I was being silly. This was rubbish. Unreasonable, obsessive madness. But I just wanted to make sure, and heading back to my old stomping ground and brushing the dust off some memories from my wild years before they slipped away from me for ever seemed like the best way to get confirmation. Also, by getting closer to The Ninny That I Used To Be, I felt I would gain a greater understanding of Peter.

Not that I told him any of this.

'Let's just say it's a virtual music journey through 1992,' I explained to him, as I pulled up the sliproad of junction 26 of the M1. 'Imagine it: Nirvana's *Nevermind* on the listening posts in Virgin Megastore, Smashing Pumpkins on *The Late Show*.'

'Cool,' said Peter. 'I don't know what *The Late Show*

is. But, like, you mean *Nevermind* will really be on the listening posts in Virgin?'

'Well, no, I doubt it. But we can do our best to pretend it is. And there'll be other things that really are *genuinely* like 1992. Such as crusties.'

'What are they?'

'Let me think of the best way to describe them . . . They're kind of like the human version of some two-week-old toast that's been left out in the rain. Not many of them exist any more, but most of the ones that do tend to linger around the stone lions in Nottingham Market Square. In 1992 they were big news. Some of them were genuinely homeless, but most of them were homeless as . . . well, I suppose as a lifestyle choice. They listened to The Levellers a lot.'

'Who are The Levellers?'

'They were a kind of pretend folk band for people who owned combat boots. They had names like Thrug and Sprout, and wrote this song which went "There's only one way of life, and that's your own". Loads of people dressed identically used to punch the air and sing along to it at my local student nightclub.'

'Ugh. Weird. But what do you mean? Like, how do you be homeless as a lifestyle choice?'

'Well, for example, there was this girl who my mate John used to go to college with. Claudia, I think she was called. She lived in one of the biggest houses in Bramcote, which is like this pretty affluent suburb of Nottingham, but on a Saturday she would rub margarine on her hair, put on a combat jacket, attach the family terrier to a piece of string and walk around the Market Square pretending to be called Mucka.'

'Why? Because she was mucky?'

'Maybe . . .'

'Is it true that if you leave your hair for long enough, it starts to wash itself? Raf said he heard it somewhere and was going to try it.'

'Er . . . I'm not sure. I heard that too, but the only person I ever knew who tried it was this kid called Nigel who went to the Nottingham Boys' High School, and I lost touch with him before the washing process had kicked in.'

'What I want to know is: does your hair condition itself, too? And if not, how do you know when to condition it? I have enough problems with conditioning mine as it is.'

'Mmm. It's a good point. But we're talking about hair again, aren't we?'

'Oh yeah. I'm growing mine at the moment.'

'I noticed. It's losing that straw mushroom thing.'

I pulled into the multi-storey car park of Nottingham's Royal Hotel. To Peter, this might have seemed like any old car park, but in fact I'd chosen it very carefully. Like the remainder of today's itinerary, it had a rock and roll history attached to it. For starters, it had been the place where I'd traditionally parked my mum and dad's rusty Seventies Toyota while attending Alternative Night across the road at the East Midlands' stickiest nightclub, Rock City. Additionally, it had been where Duran Duran had shot the inside cover photo for their *Rio* album. I thought about informing Peter of this last point, then reminded myself that I was being teenage today, and that during my adolescence I'd renounced Duran Duran as the height of uncool.

In order to get a true understanding of the way a teenager thinks, my initial idea had been to spend our Nottingham trip *being* my seventeen-year-old self. For a couple of days, I would drive like him, wear his clothes and call his old friends to invite them to Alternative Night. Peter, meanwhile, would pose as 'Pezza', my underage yet surprisingly grunge-savvy sidekick. In one sense, this was a more practical plan than one might have imagined (1992 seemed a lot less far away in Nottingham than it did in most other parts of the country), but there were the inevitable barriers.

1. I'd sold all my punk and grunge t-shirts at a flea market in 1995, in an attempt to raise funds for my first microwave.
2. Rick, of Rick Argues fame, now owned my Dead Kennedys baseball cap, and would no doubt argue if I said that I wanted it back.
3. Most of my grunge and punk friends' phone numbers were now obsolete.
4. The chain on Peter's trousers lacked grunge authenticity.
5. Alternative Night no longer existed.
6. The whole exercise would make me feel like a wanker.

There had to be another way to create our own educational time warp: it was right on the tip of my brain. I just needed to think it out. So I thought for a moment. Then, when I'd thought for a moment, I phoned Roland. It seemed kind of obvious, in retrospect.

I first met Roland in the summer of 1992, in the

moshpit of a Senseless Things gig. I was the one moshing; Roland was flailing around at my feet, having been knocked over by an overzealous crusty. I helped him up and accompanied him to the bar – surreptitiously elbowing the crusty in the back on the way – and we got talking about our mutual love of the first Smashing Pumpkins album. Over the next three years, Roland would get knocked over a lot at gigs and in nightclubs, but would always remain in even humour. In fact, in the decade that I'd known him, I'd never seen Roland in *bad* humour – or particularly good humour, for that matter – about anything. Roland looked a little like a prematurely bald version of John F. Kennedy, but, when drunk, would miraculously transmute into Bob Hoskins. Yet even this unfortunate side-effect was not enough to upset his equilibrium.

My only reservation about Roland was that, even after dozens and dozens of gigs and Alternative Nights, I didn't really feel like I knew who he was. I knew that he owned a limited edition copy of the first Stone Roses album with a much-sought-after bonus track, and I knew exactly what his favourite five Afghan Whigs b-sides were, in order, but I knew relatively little about The Real Roland: whether he was right or left wing or somewhere in the middle, whether he preferred Indian or Chinese takeaways, whether he'd ever cried after watching a sporting event, what his ambitions were, whom he fancied (who didn't happen to be in a band), whom he aspired to emulate (who didn't happen to be in a band). For Roland, music was a form of communication as well as an obsession. When you picked up the phone and said, 'Hello,' to him, he didn't say, 'Hi, how are you?', he said, without preamble, 'I've just got the new Fuckweasel album on Dogwater Records out of Ohio – limited edition pressing of two hundred and thirty-one. *Really* low-fi.'

When I split up with my girlfriend of six and a half years, most of my friends talked to me in relative depth about it and enquired as to how I was feeling, but Roland just looked nervous, mumbled something sounding vaguely like 'bummer', and asked me if I still listened to the first Superchunk album or if I thought, on balance, the third one had a greater longevity. This kind of behaviour hadn't seemed all that unusual to me back in 1993, when Roland was by no means the only male I knew whose principal form of social inter-action constituted a game of Name The Lyric, but more recently it had started to come between us, and I'd got the impression that Roland was stuck in a perpetual cycle of the Indie Rock Years, 1992–95. Call it growing apart; call it a new set of priorities; or call it the fact that Roland had pushed a few too many of my female friends off the pavement in an attempt to talk to me about God Is My Co-Pilot's unreleased demos. These days, we communicated primarily through a pair of monthly emails: the one from me, which would attempt to provide a round-up of the least mundane details of my everyday existence and make a per-functory enquiry about life in the record store where Roland held a part-time job; and the one from Roland, which would attempt to list and rank the highlights from 1993 episodes of the John Peel radio show.

Peter got on *brilliantly* with Roland.

The three of us convened, at Roland's suggestion, outside the Nottingham branch of Selectadisc, the Midlands' largest independent record shop. The idea was that we would take the afternoon to peruse the landmarks of The Indie Idiot Years, with me relating instructive anecdotes to Peter, and Roland providing ambience and such useful supporting facts as 'Yes, I believe Mudhoney were playing at the time' and 'No, I think it was actually Student Night, not Alternative Night, when that happened – I remember because we'd been to Punk Night the night before, and they'd played "This Is Radio Clash" for the first time ever'. Selectadisc seemed like a good place to start, since it had been the daytime meeting spot of ninety-nine per-cent of my social encounters between 1992 and 1994 (the night-time one being the left lion in the Market Square). Plus, if you ignored a brief period during 1998 when he became convinced that one of the sales assistants was 'looking' at him and opted to shop at QVC instead, it had been Roland's favourite shop for over ten years. Ultimately, he'd always wanted a job here, but had never quite made the grade at interview level and had had to settle for a position 'working for The Man' (I feel certain he'd prefer it if I didn't get specific about which branch of The Man), but even this monumental Life Tragedy had failed to chip away at his love for Selecta's five floors of esoteric treasures. When Roland didn't answer his phone, the easiest way to get in touch with him was usually to wait next to one of the shop's many Guided By Voices bootlegs. He'd turn up sooner or later.

It hadn't taken long for Roland and Peter to hit it off in Selectadisc and adjourn to the section marked 'US Alternative', and as we walked towards the Market Square, I found that now it was me who was getting pushed off the pavement, trying my best to earwig.

'So, you really think "Vegative Creep" is better than "Breed"? . . . Interesting,' Roland was saying to Peter, with an arched eyebrow.

'It's just, y'know, heavier,' shrugged Peter.

'But I always thought it was a commonly held opinion that "Breed" represented the pinnacle of Cobain's angst, yet married to a pop sensibility. But then I suppose it would have been even, y'know, cooler if it had had Albini producing.'

Roland was always saying things like 'represented the pinnacle of Cobain's angst, yet married to a pop sensibility'. When I'd packed in writing for the *New Musical Express* in 1997 and declared to Roland that the paper was by and large run by identikit indie élitists getting revenge for having their lunchboxes stolen at school, he'd looked at me as if I'd just insulted his mother, and, I suspected, had never quite been able to bring himself to view me as a full human being since.

'Do you like Suede?' he asked Peter now.

'Nnhgh. Er. I think so.'

'What do you think of Brett Anderson's ambiguous sexuality?'

'Not sure. I guess it's cool. He's got good hair, I suppose.'

'He once said he was a bisexual who'd never had a

homosexual experience. I guess it was a publicity stunt, but it was kind of a cool thing to say.'

'Yeah. Er. Yeah, I suppose.'

'Tom says you live in London. Do you get many good indie nights there?'

'I dunno. I'm a bit too, like, young to get into them. I get into pubs sometimes, though. And I did go and see Kitty at this really cool place where you didn't have to be eighteen.'

'Kitty? Mmm. Are they a bit like L7?'

'Who are L7? I *think* I've heard of them.'

'Didn't you see them on *The Word*? One of them took her pants down. It was soooo cool. I remember it well: 26 November 1992. Around eleven minutes to ten. Tom used to like stuff like that – I mean, he used to own the first Babes In Toyland EP. But now he listens to all that Seventies stuff. I mean – ha! – what an indie traitor. A lot of the stuff he listens to now is, like, the sort of stuff they play in Asda!'

A bus hurtled along Market Street, splashing muddy water up the back of my cardigan and forcing me further back up the hill. I didn't catch the next thing Peter and Roland said, but as I returned to their side they were laughing conspiratorially.

We'd reached the Market Square. Disappointingly, there weren't any crusties about, although I did spot the first Ned's Atomic Dustbin t-shirt I'd seen since 1993. As I attempted to find somewhere to sit between the pigeon shit on the steps near the left lion, and watched Roland assiduously examining the print on the back of Peter's Nirvana t-shirt, I reflected that I'd come about as far from my idea of a horizon-expanding road trip as possible. I couldn't even see a horizon. I was back in my home town, it was raining, I had a cold coming on, I couldn't find a crusty to ridicule, I'd long since given up on my one attempt at a rock-and-roll form of transport, and I felt seventeen again. The last of these facts at least spoke of some sense of wish fulfilment, but was nonetheless difficult to find solace in.

'So,' I sniffed in Peter's general direction, 'picture the scene: a typical Thursday night in 1992. Hundreds of teenagers in ridiculous stripey grandad tops, all purchased from the same alternative boutique, and para boots, all purchased from the same army surplus store, descend on the left lion, then filter off to the city's three non-townie-populated pubs, before dancing away their cares at Rock City's Student Night.'

'Nnngh,' said Peter. 'Then what happens?'

'Well – er, nothing, a lot of the time. We'd all drink watered-down beer, some of us would ogle girls in PJ Harvey t-shirts but not do anything about it, and Roland would get pushed over. Then, when it was over, I'd drive really fast down the ramps at the multi-storey car park across the road.'

'Oh,' said Peter.

'Tom, you make it sound like I always fell over,' said Roland. 'I mean, be fair – it was only once or twice.'

'Yeah. Per *week*.'

I'd be lying if I said I felt completely proud of my late teenage years, but I had hoped that, given an impressionable audience, I'd be able to paint them in a romantic, fantastical light as my own minor but perfectly formed response to a rebel adolescence in late-Sixties Haight-Ashbury or late-Eighties

Manchester. Now, though, I discovered it wasn't going to be as easy as I'd hoped to inject the necessary amount of glamour into the re-enactment of The Year That Grunge Broke, Midlands-style. The more scenarios I tried to recreate, the more intensely Peter seemed to examine the packet of French fries he'd bought. And Roland wasn't proving to be as useful a prop as I'd hoped either, chipping in with plenty of stories about some indie band or other that I'd orphaned, but consistently failing to back me up on what I considered to be the day's most action-packed stories.

'Do you remember what happened here?' I asked him later, as we pulled up outside my old college.

'No. What?' he said.

'You know. When I was driving everyone to college and I went across the grass for a laugh . . .'

'Nope. Don't know what you're talking about.'

'Oh, come on! The car spinning out of control, the boot of that Mini looming in the wing mirror, all of us ending up in the ditch. Surely you remember! We all agreed it was a life-changing experience. All eight of us.'

'Neh.'

'Anyway,' I said, swallowing my irritation and turning to Peter, 'the lesson here is not to drive while listening to the New Bomb Turks. Too much automatic adrenalin.'

'Right,' said Peter.

'First album or second album?' asked Roland.

'First,' I said. 'I don't think the second one was out by then.'

'*Now* I remember,' said Roland.

For four hours or more, the three of us zig-zagged across Greater Nottingham, analysing my murky past and Roland's only slightly less murky present. For each case study there was a story and a music-related lesson for Peter. Outside an office building that used to be a pub called The Narrowboat, there was the story of when a crap new wave of new wave band forgot that I was supposed to be interviewing them for my fanzine and left me sitting in the corner of their dressing room feeling scared (the lesson: don't interview crap new wave of new wave bands). Outside my college radio room, there was the story of how me and my mate Surreal Ed were supposed to be broadcasting an American indie rock show to a ten-mile radius, then didn't (the lesson: don't imagine that college lecturers who use the phrase 'Let's have a brainstorm and address the problem' a lot will help further your musical career). Outside the Forte Crest Hotel, there was the story of how I'd failed to get a snog off a beautiful Spanish woman by not knowing the lyrics to the second verse of REM's 'Losing My Religion' (the lesson: never underestimate the pulling power of sensitive ballads). And outside Marks and Spencer, there was the story of the time that Roland, accompanying me on a college radio project, asked a blind saxophone-playing busker what he thought of Brett Anderson's ambiguous sexuality (the lesson: don't talk indie crap to a blind busker).

Of course, whether any of these case studies had any relevance to Peter – or to an education in the real values of rock and roll – was very much up for debate.

He was, after all, fourteen, not seventeen, but I felt that a journey inside my seventeen-year-old psyche was relevant, since a) Peter was advanced for his age, and b) the primary music-themed lesson from my fourteen-year-old psyche would have to be drawn from the somewhat limited source that was the theme tune to my *Nick Faldo's Golf Course* video. Again, I didn't tell him this. In the endless comparisons I'd made between Peter's adolescence and mine, I'd never properly explained to him how desperately golf-obsessed and musically ignorant I'd been when I was his age. It would have taken far too long, and making the assumption that Peter now and myself at seventeen were one and the same seemed a good, lazy way of flattering him.

I just wished he'd *act* a little more flattered.

During the course of the afternoon, the cement had hardened on the union between Peter and Roland, and, while it was Roland who was doing most of the uniting, I could feel Peter drifting away from me again. I'm sure my habit of popping into Waterstones and Habitat between case studies and leaving the two of them outside, in the way that you might a couple of disgruntled pet dogs, wasn't helping. But even without that indulgence, the anti-Tom propaganda would probably have been building at a similarly steady rate. From what I could overhear, most of this bitching seemed to be fairly harmless – thin-skinned or thick-skinned, it's hard to feel genuinely hurt when someone's main basis for grousing about you behind your back is the fact that you don't listen to Half Man Half Biscuit any more – but I was starting to think that maybe I'd slipped up by inviting Roland on this section of our adventure. Before today, I'd been keen to show Peter that I hadn't always been a boring adult. Now, not only did I feel like Roland was detracting from that, I also felt he was *seriously* detracting from one of the main lessons that I'd always thought, in order to fulfil my favour to Jenny properly, was essential to Peter's studies: the lesson that said there was more to life than music.

'I mean, it's obvious,' Roland told Peter, as we passed Langtry's, a pub I'd once been thrown out of for pulling the stuffing out of a chair. 'If you like U2, you're a twat. Have you ever met anyone you enjoy spending time with who likes U2?'

'I'm not sure,' said Peter.

'*Of course you haven't!* All twats. It's the same with Pearl Jam. Liking Pearl Jam is, by definition, a sure sign of twat-hood. They are now, and always have been, the sell-out's answer to Nirvana. How can you like them and not be an idiot?'

'But I like U2. And Pearl Jam have done some alright stuff, too,' I said.

'Yeah, but you're different, Tom,' said Roland. 'You're just saying that for effect. One day you'll come back to your indie roots, and I'll be there to say I told you so.'

'Yeah,' I said. 'Actually, Roland, you're right. I can see that happening because, y'know, it's loads more fun listening to bands who sound like something faulty you bought from Comet than listening to bands who write melodies and stuff. Music's not just something you wear as a badge, Roland.'

'Reactionary,' said Roland.

'Bigot,' I said.

'I like Rammstein,' said Peter.

Over the last ten years, Roland and I had had countless conversations like this one. This disagreement
wouldn't change the way either of us thought. The
next time I saw him, probably in several months, we'd
still be friends, in a circumspect kind of way. Roland
would still ask me why I didn't listen to Polvo any
more and, while he wasn't looking, I'd still write 'I
love REO Speedwagon!' on his rucksack. That said,
right now, the whole episode bugged the shit out of me.
It was dispiriting to think that earlier I'd actually looked
forward to being seventeen for a day – that I'd imagined
it might involve fun things like climbing on scaffolding
and insulting crusties, rather than going round in tiny-
minded circles arguing about rock music.

I'd been thinking about my relationship with Roland
a lot recently. That was one of the side-effects of
spending time with Peter: it got me musing wistfully
about the nature of human change and friendships. I'd
probably lost touch with friends I had more in
common with than Roland over the years, yet the two
of us chose to hold on, even though the only thing that
seemed to bind us was the albums we'd taped for one
another a decade ago – albums that, with the odd
exception, I didn't even like any more. The relationship might have seemed somewhat odd to an outsider,
but it probably seemed odder to me. Peter, however,
didn't seem to think it was bizarre in the slightest.

'I liked him,' he told me later, after we'd dropped
Roland home.

'I don't think he likes *me* much any more,' I said.

'Really? I didn't notice.'

'But surely you saw how much we argued about stuff?'

'I thought that was kind of normal.'

'For us, it is.'

'He seemed kind of younger than you.'

'Really? I mean, in what way? He's bald!'

'Mmm, I know. But he just didn't talk about adult stuff like you do.'

'What kind of adult stuff? You mean porn?'

'No! I mean, y'know, how if we're driving past a forest with some sheep in front of it or something, you'll say, "What a great view." Or when we've left your house sometimes, you say stuff like, "I hope I didn't leave the coffee machine on." I can't imagine Roland saying stuff like that.'

'No. Neither can I. I see what you mean. He still lives with his mum and dad – that might be something to do with it.'

'No way! I hope I don't still live with my mum when I'm his age. I want to be out of there by the time I'm seventeen.'

'That's quite early.'

'Yeah. Goat Punishment are all going to get a house together.'

'What? Like The Monkees?'

'Not really.'

'Do you feel like you've learned anything today?'

'I dunno. Er. I'm not sure. I kind of like it better when you write stuff down, when you're telling me about what you did when you were younger.'

'So there was nothing you felt you really learned.'

'I wouldn't say "learned" was the right word. Er . . . Roland liked Smashing Pumpkins. That was cool.'

'Yeah. He likes their first album. It's one of the few things we both still like from our Alternative Night days.'

'Mmm. Yeah. I'm taping him their latest one . . . when I buy it, which is going to be really soon.'

'You took his address?'

'Yeah.'

'So you might end up being friends? That's good.'

'I dunno. Maybe.'

'It's weird. I really wish I had more in common with him these days. I mean, I've never really talked to him about girls or anything, apart from when he used to go on about the lead singer of Velocity Girl. It's like music's the one thing that holds us together. Do you have any mates that you feel like that about?'

'I suppose it's a bit like that with Raf.'

'But you mess around together and jump around on space hoppers. I never really did stuff like that with Roland. I did that with my other mates, and they've never really got on with him. I mean, if you and Raf didn't have music, what would you have left?'

'Mmm. I'm not sure. I guess I'd have to think about that . . .'

He went silent for a few minutes. I thought he looked troubled, but I couldn't be sure. Like so many other times with Peter, I hoped I hadn't got too deep with him and given him too much perspective on the kind of things that being a happy teenager is all about failing to dwell on. This teaching business, I reflected, was a difficult balancing act: how did you find the happy middle ground between too little knowledge and too much knowledge? I worried to myself briefly and scrambled for a less reflective conversation topic, but within a few moments Peter was back from wherever he'd drifted off to, taking pleasure in breaking into a tub of Cadbury's Heroes he'd purchased from a newsagent down the road from my old FE college. Suddenly enlightenment broke across his face – something truly revitalising to be a part of. Apparently, he'd never liked miniature Bounties, and now, as if answering his prayers, the manufacturers had ceased to include them.

SMASHING PUMPKINS –
MACHINA/MACHINES OF GOD
(HOT RECORDS, 2000)

Tom: 'For the dizzy hippy posing as disaffected slacker, Smashing Pumpkins were the perfect band to help you dream your way through the grunge era. Their debut album, *Gish*, which came out on the same day in 1991 as Nirvana's *Nevermind*, has been portrayed since as a kind of 'Neverwas', but it would have been an ill-adapted flagship album for grunge, more concerned with insects, wildlife and what colour beads to wear than with hating its parents and exploring the catacombs of existential doom. *Gish* was the sound of Black Sabbath on their backs in the Garden of Eden. Had it been the album that introduced grunge to the mainstream, Marilyn Manson, Offspring, Green Day mark two, and every other snivelling American oh-look-how-fucked-up-I-am-my-mum's-cut-off-my-pocket-money excuse for a musician might never have existed. Imagine how much less irritating "alternative" teenagers might be today with the solid foundation of an album with no discernible messages other than "chill out", "rock hard", "cool sweater, dude" and "hey – look at that fluorescent rhinoceros in the sky".

'In the event, however, the scandalous underperformance of *Gish* did almost as much harm to the Smashing Pumpkins as the overperformance of *Nevermind* did to a generation of disaffected mid-Nineties teens. While grunge begat complaint rock, which begat shock rock and my-dad's-an-accountant-but-feel-my-pain rock, the dreamy Pumpkins of *Gish* were replaced by self-righteous humanoids – a band who, since 1995, have done almost as much as anyone to endorse the commodification of self-loathing. "Despite all my rage, I'm just a rat in the cage!" they whined at middle-America. For reasons beyond human comprehension, they sold by the skipload.

'The progress of Smashing Pumpkins over their last three albums – 1995's *Melon Collie And The Infinite Sadness*, 1998's *Adore* and *Machina/Machines Of God* – is similar to that of a laggard juggernaut attempting to manoeuvre out of an unusually tight parking space: a little bit forwards, a little backwards, a little sideways, but never more than a few inches in any direction. Compared to *Adore* (which exhibited singer Billy Corgan's gruesome Eighties electro-rock obsession), *Machina* must be considered a slender move forwards, striving to recycle the pompous, transparent fury of *Melon Collie*, but with one wheel stuck in 1987, some-where in the middle of a Mission b-side.

'There are hints of the old Pumpkins here: "Stand Inside Your Love" could almost be a rewrite of "Cherub Rock" from 1993's *Siamese Dream* album, and "With Every Light" is a distant, shrivelled relation to *Gish*'s "Snail". But Billy Corgan, The Professional Awkward Sod Who Looks Like The "Monster-Monster" Bloke From *The Fast Show,* probably can't even remember Billy Corgan, The Intriguing Bohemian Freak With The Pink Hair. Besides, why would he want to remember a time when no-one told him he was any good, when he's so comfortable in the present, surrounded – no doubt – by legions of yes-men?

'As the Pumpkins fluctuate between death fuzz ("The Everlasting Gaze"), plod whinge ("Try Try Try") and cod prog ("Glass And The Ghost Children"), the root formula – over-coddled corporate goth-grunge – doesn't change. The Pumpkins are now so million-dollar tried'n'tested that Corgan could put out an album of a cappella farmyard noises and receive his record company's unconditional seal of approval. In fact, after *Machina*, it's probably the next logical step.

'The voice here is always the biggest hurdle: wailing, indulging, never giving its musical accompaniment chance to breathe, it manages to be both totally self-conscious and totally unaware of its own absurdity. The negative energy is immense, polluting the atmosphere for seventy-plus minutes without defining a source or hinting at a destination. Unlike early Smashing Pumpkins, who said ostensibly nothing but could be construed to mean a million things if listened to with the right amount of imagination, this band are patently bored, overindulged and, all in all, a bit like the half-friend you used to have who played the role of manic depressive purely for attention and out of fear that, if they chilled out, their non-personality might be revealed. Ignore them, and they might go away.'

Peter: 'My mate Sam – he's like the second best guitar player in school, after Raf? – taped this for me. I couldn't believe I hadn't heard it before. I mean, I should have – it's weird that I hadn't read stuff about them in *Kerrang!*, 'cos I read that all the time, or used to, it's gone a bit crap now. Anyway, they look a bit weird – that bloke who looks like the monster guy from *The Fast Show*, and the oriental bloke with the long hair, I thought he was a girl at first – but they're really amazing musicians. The drumming is just . . . out there. The guitars remind me of squealing gerbils some-times. Sort of goth, but sort of so . . . bizarre and more electronic than stuff I normally listen to. Not dance, though. I hate dance music. Me and Raf have formed this group outlawing dance. That's what it's called – Group Outlawing Dance. But we write the logo as God. But, yeah, that girl, D'Arcy, who plays guitar? Rhythm, I think. I think the bald guy plays lead. She's fit. Sam has a picture of her taped to his Humanities folder. None of the girls in my year could ever look as cool as that, even when they're, like, seventeen or eighteen. I haven't got their other albums yet, but I'm going to get them now. Probably tomorrow. I dunno. It depends if my mum can pick me up from fencing or if I have to go home on the bus. Anyway – soon. Wicked. Nine and three quarters out of ten.'

Tom: 'Why did you knock a quarter mark off? I thought you were going to give it ten.'

Peter: 'That *Fast Show* guy gives me the creeps a bit, that's all.'

EDUCATING
PETER **CHEATING**

During the week following our Nottingham trip, I emailed Peter to ask what he'd thought of a compilation tape I'd loaned to him, 'Tom's Peasant Island Discs 1993'. Much as I would have liked to deny it, I found email a much easier form of pan-generational communication than the telephone – not to mention a simpler way of getting feedback out of my pupil. In short: it was hard work to grunt via computer.

Peter's emails were terser than those of most of my other friends, dispensing with such pleasantries as 'Hi', 'What have you been up to?' and 'Best Wishes', but at least he made good use of the subject box and expressed himself in something approaching intelligible English. Whereas on the phone he might have gone into monosyllabic mode, paused for uncomfortably long periods and failed to express that, say, he'd enjoyed 'There Is A Light That Never Goes Out' by The Smiths, email seemed to loosen him up, giving his inner cultural commentator the forum for expression that it had been longing for. Either that, or he'd just really liked my tape. Peter might have failed to listen to a lot of the music I'd steered in his direction, but I had to give him his due: when he did listen to something, he *really* listened to it. In much the same way that I'd hoped *The Best Of Grand Funk Railroad* would, 'Tom's Peasant Island Discs 1993', with its selection of forgotten leftfield rockers and bed-sit poets, had really struck a chord with him, and before long he was quoting the soundtrack of my idiot years back to me. It was the kind of thing that, had I been Jim Eldon, would probably have had me blubbing into my keyboard, and I wished I could reciprocate by quoting from 'This CD Will Self-Destruct', the CD that Peter had made for me of his favourite nu-metal songs. Regrettably, though, my hearing wasn't sharp enough to penetrate its sludge-laden guitars and Yeti-like bellowing.

'I quite like the Kyuss track: it's got a sort of stoner rock feel,' I wrote of Peter's CD. 'Reminds me of Blue Cheer. But I'm not so sure about the one by Drowning Pool. It frightened the cats a bit. And why do Kyuss keep singing about bodies hitting the floor?'

'It's just a song about death and destruction,' Peter wrote in response. 'It's cool. But I think "Eyeless" by Slipknot is the coolest. I like that lyric: "You can't see California without Marlon Brando's eyes".'

'What does it mean?' I wrote.

'I don't know,' wrote Peter. 'It's just really ... thoughtful.'

Peter's emails didn't just feature regurgitated lyrics; they also featured impenetrable slogans and surreal statements of a totally non-music-related nature: isolated sentences, occasionally of an unnervingly political inclination, bearing no relation to the remainder of the email. These tended to confuse me, and leave me feeling uncertain as to whether or not I was required to respond to them. Examples included:

'What do Hiroshima, Nagasaki and Baghdad have in common? Nothing . . . Yet.'

'Salute the carrot.'

'Open the gates. What's inside? DARKNESS.'

'Icons are like shoes: a matter of opinion.'

'Blair, Bush, bomb: things that begin with B. Question: what begins with Z?'

And perhaps most perplexingly of all:

'If a cauliflower is a dog in the animal world, what colour, in an ideal world, is a tree?'

Was Peter reaching out to me in some obscure way? I wondered. Maybe. Was he trying to get me involved in a deep philosophical discussion? Perhaps. But more likely he was just fulfilling another part of his hormonal destiny. In the end I decided it best to ignore his statements. I would probably only have had to go back to South Nottinghamshire College and read the ancient biro inscriptions on the rubber desks to find that I, too, had once felt the need to expose the wider universe to my deeper, more surreal thoughts. And what had that signified? Precisely nothing. Ten years on, what was I? An apolitical Steve Miller Band fan whose most profound daily 'statement' involved inventing stupid names for his cats.

The other strange thing about Peter's emails was something I didn't notice until perhaps the third or fourth communication in the wake of the Nottingham trip. It was to do with the way he signed off:

'Laters,

Petter'

I understood the 'Laters' bit. Even I was still hip enough to realise that this was an insouciant young person's way of saying, 'Goodbye, take care, and – you know what? – I'm really going to miss you!'; it wasn't unheard of for people my age (people my age in complicated athletic footwear, anyway) to use it. What I didn't understand was the bit below it. Had Peter changed his name without telling me? Or was it possible that in all our time together I'd been spelling it wrong? Not wishing to hurt his feelings, I approached Jenny about the matter.

'Oooh yes. I've been meaning to talk to you about that. He's decided to have a little bit of a change,' said Jenny.

'What? So he's called Petter now? Isn't that Swedish?' I said.

'No. You don't pronounce it "Petter". One of the "t"s is silent.'

'I don't get it. What's the point?'

'Well, to be honest, I think he's a bit cheesed off at having such a normal name. You know, all his mates have these unusual names like Zed and Raf and Jonti. He's always having a go at me about it, so I figured, What the hell?, let him add a letter to it. He'll probably grow out of it. I think, really, it's just a bit fashionable to spell words in a weird way. There's the band, isn't there – what are they called? – Staind, but without an "e". And there's the other one. I think they're called

Soil but they have a "d" at the end. I called them Soiled and he got very angry with me and started doing that stomping thing on the stairs on the way to his room.'

'Actually, I think they are just called Soil, without the "d". At least, that's how he's written it on "This CD Will Self-Destruct".'

'On what?'

'Oh, the compilation CD he made for me. It's very professionally done. He even drew his own "Parental Advisory" sticker on it.'

'Oh, one of *those* things. I sometimes think manu- facturers only stick those on to sell more records.'

The next time I saw Petter, I opted to keep quiet about his new moniker. Going by what Jenny had said, it was clearly a sensitive issue, and I didn't want to do anything to detract from the new level of musical understanding we'd reached. Despite what Roland might have had you believe, I still felt secretly proud of 'Tom's Peasant Island Discs 1993'. When I'd fished it out of an old box in my parents' attic at the begin- ning of the year, I'd been surprised – considering just how much unlistenable hogwash I'd pretended to like as an eighteen-year-old – at the quality of its track selection. Astonishingly, it didn't feature one band that sounded remotely like a broken dishwasher or some furniture falling down some stairs. Sure, I would have been happier if Petter had joined me in my love of Led Zeppelin and Lynyrd Skynyrd, but never- theless, having him join me in my old – and, in a small way, still burgeoning – love of early Madder Rose and Pavement singles represented a bona fide result. I felt, for the first time, as though I was only a few short steps away from gaining a better understanding of my pupil's musical universe.

'This CD Will Self-Destruct' took me a tiny bit closer. It might have mystified me, but between all the growling, thundering, dying and destructing, I could find the beginning of a line of musical aesthetics and trace it back, if not to my old self, then at least to some people my old self had been slightly intimidated by. What Petter listened to still scared me, but at root it was surely just a slightly heavier version of what the DJs at Rock City's Alternative Night used to play, with more dying in it. It reminded me of a specific breed of alternative rock fan I used to know: slightly hairier than the people I used to hang around with, and almost certainly with bigger shorts. But most of all, it reminded me of the Reading Festival.

Ten years ago, the Reading Festival had been Britain's second biggest annual outdoor rock event: a less mellowed-out, smellier rival to the Glastonbury Festival. These days, it was still enormously popular, but seemed to have lost its personality somewhat. Or perhaps I was just out of touch. Whatever the case, I was pretty sure that, in late August, Reading town centre would be full of people who looked just like older versions of Petter. I was also sure that Petter would jump at the chance of being there and feel even greater respect for me as a tutor if I was the one to offer him his first taste – and, more to the point, smell – of festival life.

I hadn't attended the Reading Festival as a punter since 1995, chiefly because I'd been put off music festivals for ever after one particularly dismal Glastonbury where, on the same day that I'd had my wallet pilfered, one of my friends had been mugged and another had had his tent stolen. Since then I'd been to Reading a couple of times for reviewing purposes, but never for more than a day, and always with the emphasis on clean, comfortable people-watching in the backstage area rather than on getting crushed in the moshpit next to the *Melody Maker* stage. Possessing no desire to sit in a muddy field watching metalheads paint their faces and sing along to Smurf songs in an ironic fashion, I had no intention of going back on my anti-festival stance now. Instead, I decided, I would take Petter to Reading on the day *after* the festival. By doing this I would a) avoid having my eardrums punished by Amen, Slipknot and Incubus, and b) give him the opportunity to see the day-lit downside of spending four nights without sleep in a field full of people shouting 'Bollocks!' at the top of their voices for the hell of it. Yet, simul-taneously, he would be grateful, in the special way that only a fourteen-year-old being plunged into a scene of chaos, alcoholic abandon and ear-splitting music can be.

In a sense, I was using Reading as a pay-off. A couple of days before we arrived there, I'd taken Petter to Peacehaven, near Brighton, to meet Bob Copper, the head of The Copper Family, a folk group whose story could be traced back well over a hundred years. The trip had been tough going on Petter. A few miles past Crawley he'd started to complain of a headache. I'd initially assumed that his discomfort could be entirely attributed to Crawley, or at least to the grating a cappella sounds of *Come Write Me Down*, the Copper

Family album that was playing on the Focus's stereo. I'd convinced him that he'd be fine once we'd stopped for a Burger King, and that there was no need to turn back. But I'd made an error of judgement. Around Rottingdean, with the Copper Family CD on its second rotation, Petter had spoken sharply to me for the first time ever and asked for the music to be switched off, and I'd realised he was in genuine pain. He'd also expressed a wish to wait in the car and read *Kerrang!* while I spoke to Bob.

'Are you sure?' I'd asked him.

'Yeah,' he'd mumbled. 'My brain feels like a goat farted in it. I don't think any folk's going to help at this point. All those songs about "drinking a pile of ale" — it's too much.'

'But I thought you liked booze now.'

'Yeah. But that doesn't mean I want to hear a bunch of old men sing songs about it.'

Locating Bob's ancient storybook cottage in the middle of a decidedly non-ancient, non-storybook housing estate, I steeled myself for another slightly futile encounter in the absence of my student. Fortunately, Bob was in his late eighties and seemed to have forgotten that I'd said I'd be interviewing him with a teenager in tow. A former shepherd, he had a fascinating life story, which he was eager to tell, and had home-baked some rather tasty cookies, only a few of which had his wiry grey hairs embedded in them. At one point, he even sang me a song about ale. But to be truthful, my eye was on the clock and my mind was on the ailing Petter. I'd been with Bob an hour, and he'd only reached 1957. I dearly wished I could stay longer, but I could feel my duty as a guardian over-taking my duty as a musical historian, and I made my excuses, stashing a couple of cookies in my coat for my poorly friend.

Reading was a far easier study proposition. For a start, it only had a couple of decades of history, as opposed to umpteen. Not only that, very little of this history involved sheep (although there was no deny-ing the profusion of ale). Petter hadn't really blamed me for taking him to Peacehaven and exposing him to the delights of indigenous, ancient folk music, or at least had forgiven me from the moment I'd mentioned Reading, and as I steered the Focus through the throng of Slipknot t-shirts and matted hair running parallel to the festival grounds, he seemed in higher spirits than ever.

'Did you see that?' he said. 'It was this really cool Jimmy Eat World shirt. Long-sleeved! One I've never seen before. This guy who looked like the kid from *Third Rock From The Sun* was wearing it.'

'No,' I said. 'I missed it. I was too busy trying not to run over that guy in the road.'

'What guy in the road?'

'That one there. The one lying down.'

'Oh yeah. Shit. Is he dead?'

'No. I think he's just passed out. You can see his hand twitching towards that can of Red Stripe.'

'Oh yeah.'

'He's a big fella.'

'Yeah. I don't understand how people get that fat. I don't know why, but I never seem to get on with fat people.'

'Perhaps that's because they're jealous of you, eating all those crisps but never putting on any weight.'

'Mmm. I dunno. Hey. It was really funny . . .'

'Hold on. This is a tricky bit . . .'

'Shit. Did he—'

'Nearly run into the back of me? Yeah. He did. Ridiculous, isn't it? Riding a bike when there are all these defenceless cars around. Very dangerous. Especially when you're giving a croggy to a goth girl.'

'A what?'

'A croggy.'

'What's one of them?'

'You know – where you have someone on the back of your bike.'

'Oh. We call them seaties where we come from.'

'That's a bit crap.'

'No. Croggy's crapper.'

'We'll agree to disagree on that one. Anyway, carry on . . .'

'Yeah. So . . . it was really funny. One time when we were doing Physical Ed at school, there's this fat guy – Colin? – and I don't really get on with him, but Raf does, and it's so funny 'cos Raf starts using him as this human trampoline, and throwing this really small kid – Nero? – at him and he just keeps bouncing off.'

'What? The fat kid was lying on the ground?'

'No, just like leaning against the wall. But he still had a lot of, er, bounce.'

'So why don't you get on with him?'

'Oh, he said *The Crow* was a shit film.'

'But I said that too, when I first met you.'

'Mmmm. Yeah. I guess. But that's different.'

Outside Reading train station, the t-shirts, rucksacks and sleeping bags were queuing up around the block. Sandwiched in between them were some of the sleepiest, most starey eyes you could find outside of a hypnotist's convention. Surely it would take a week to clear all these people, and at least twice as long to rejuvenate their spirits. Some of them yawned, some picked unidentified granules from their armpits, some just stared at the vehicles on the adjacent road longingly, like eighteenth-century savages contemplating space travel. I felt certain that, in two or three years, Petter would be among them.

It suddenly struck me that I'd never seen queues this long – moreover, that I'd never really been fully exposed to this end of the festival experience at all. I'd always left festivals a little bit early as the result of an argument with a girlfriend, or a stolen wallet, or a stomach problem, or a Levellers headlining slot. In short: I was always a bit of a wimp. Now, though, I could hardly say I regretted it.

Slowly – because we were walking against the vast flow of human traffic – Petter and I made our way back to the festival site from our city centre parking spot. It felt odd, being cleanly showered in the middle of all this organic body paste, and I'm sure our shiny skin would have elicited funny looks if the punters travelling in the opposite direction had possessed the energy to dole them out. There was a pungent aroma in the air – a mixture of pot and potty – and to take my mind off it I indulged Petter in a game of Spot The Band T-shirt (Slipknot won). Part of me wished Roland was here: it had always been one of his favourite pastimes.

Now I might be speaking a little rashly here, having never cleaned up in the wake of a nuclear war, but there's nothing quite like seeing a festival site the day after a major rock event. Even a freshly evacuated Evel Knievel run could not have matched it for wanton devastation. Of course, it isn't quite so shocking if you've been *at* the festival and experienced the deterioration of your body in tandem with that of the turf beneath you. But Petter and I were thrust into this apocalyptic panorama straight from the everyday, sweet(er)-smelling outside world, and it hit us hard.

Well, it hit *me* hard. Petter seemed to quite enjoy it.

'This is so cool!' he exclaimed. 'They didn't even ask us to pay at the gate.'

'Well, they couldn't, really, could they? I mean, what would they have said if we'd asked who was playing? "An old baseball boot with a hole in the toe, supported by an empty baked bean can with a dead Rizla stuffed inside." '

It was remarkable what you could find in the wake of a festival. There were the usual festival leftovers, of course: the forlorn, dust-caked bucket hats, the torn-up programmes, the ripped sleeping bags. But, as Petter and I ventured further beyond the main arena and adjusted our eyes to the carnage, the objects on the ground became more esoteric, until finally we couldn't resist putting them into a top ten of unusualness. This process involved a small amount of disagreement, but eventually could be narrowed down to:

10. A tyre.

   9. A Downfall box, empty except for a tiny toy squirrel.

8. An Action Man.

7. Two half-inflated footballs, sellotaped together, with eye-balls drawn on them.

6. Three brassieres, hooked together to form a wobbly triangle.

5. A crumpled picture of the American punk band The Strokes with a cut-out of Shannon Doherty's face pasted over the lead singer's head.

4. A Cabbage Patch Doll.

3. Many crushed cans of Stella Artois, arranged to spell the phrase 'Talk to the hand 'cos the face ain't listening'.

2. A bag of cat litter.

1. A Teasmade.

You had to marvel at the decision-making processes that had brought these objects here. People frequently did surreal things at festivals and revived obscure items from their past – a case in point would be the night during the 1994 festival when, out of nowhere, the thirty tents nearest mine had all shouted, 'Bob Carolgees and his dog Spit!' in unison – but that still didn't explain why, while packing his rucksack, some-one would have thought, I know: I better take some cat litter. Because, well, you never know, do you? I didn't like The Strokes and I thought Cabbage Patch Dolls were hideous, but I still felt sad that they had to die here, defaced and unloved.

Unlike Glastonbury, which was held in a genuinely charismatic place, the Reading Festival site, without all the crowds and the noise, was an eyesore: a few very ordinary fields overlooking some even more ordinary car dealerships and a leisure centre straight out of *The Alan Partridge Book Of Architecture*. It was all rather frustrating. Over the last few months I'd driven Petter through some truly beautiful, and sometimes spectacular, English countryside: he'd been over the Humber Bridge, he'd travelled the coast road to Hastings, and he'd hung out in a tree in Oxley's Wood. But it was here, of all places, that he walked around with his head up, breathing in his surroundings like an old-time country squire recovering from cabin fever.

'Look at the size of that mixing desk!' he marvelled, as we passed by the main arena.

'Yeah,' I said. 'The traditional thing at Reading is to say to your mates, "Meet you by the mixing desk." It looks quite easy now, but at nine o'clock on a Saturday night it's virtually impossible. Also it's quite dark. You might think you've met your friend, but actually discover later that you've gone back to your tent with a forty-three-year-old Paul Weller fan from Southampton.'

'When I meet Raf at the weekend sometimes, we say we'll meet each other outside HMV in the West End. But we always forget to say which branch and end up going to different ones . . . Ugh. What's that?'

'I think it's some kind of bandage.'

'But that's blood inside it.'

'Yeah. Horrible. Weird things happen in this field. I camped in this one in 1994. A drug dealer unzipped my tent in the middle of the night and tried to sell me speed. Then the next night, me and my girlfriend had gone to bed and there was this creature outside talking to our friends. I couldn't tell if it was male or female.

It had this voice like someone had swabbed the inside of its throat with meths. Someone probably had. Later it fell on our tent and broke it.'

'Weird.'

'No. Just annoying, really. You see that? That's where they had the bungee jump in 1995. I remember one person getting up there and then not being able to go through with it. The whole site was yelling "JUMP!" at him.'

'My neck's really sore.'

'Why? You haven't been bungee jumping, have you?'

'Oh. No. Just headbanging.'

'Why do you do it, then?'

'I dunno. There's no real point to gigs if you don't, is there? And it was Slipknot yesterday. It wasn't like I was going to stand at the back and not go into the moshpit.'

'What do you mean, "yesterday"?'

'They were here, on the main stage.'

'You came here yesterday, to the festival?'

'Mmmm. Yeah. My dad brought us here. Me, Raf, Zed and this girl – Caroline? My dad watched Slipknot, too. I think he quite liked them. But I think he liked Incubus best. He said so anyway. I'm not sure if he'd, like, put them on in his spare time or anything.'

'Oh. Right . . . I see.'

'It was really funny, yeah? Caroline had just got back from Thailand and she was still really jetlagged. People kept seeing her and thinking she was stoned. And then we were in the moshpit, and there was this real mosher there, and him and Raf were, like, lifting one another up and then crowdsurfing. It was really violent. I've got such a cool bruise on my shin.'

'What, so you camped and everything?'

'No. We stayed at Caroline's auntie's house in Oxford. Caroline's, like, sooo bayse.'

'So *what*?'

'Bayse. You know.'

'No. I don't know. What does it mean?'

'It's kind of like what you say about people who are well off, but kind of dozey.'

'Why didn't you tell me any of this before?'

'What? About being bayse?'

'No. The festival.'

'Dunno. Didn't think it was important.'

'I'm sort of surprised you want to be back here today, after seeing the real thing yesterday.'

'No. It's cool. I wanted to see if I could find the patch where Raf was sick.'

'Oh. Where was that?'

'Just over there, by the burger stall. I guess some-one's cleared it up by now.'

As we walked back towards the car, the crowd had thinned out slightly. A few stragglers sat on street corners, perched on empty beer crates and rolled-up sleeping bags, with the look of people who were wait-ing for something but couldn't quite remember what. I chose not to act on Petter's suggestion that we 'give them all a lift'. I'd only just valeted the car, for a start, and besides, I was feeling slightly sore at my Nordically named companion. Whether or not he'd made a premeditated decision to withhold the fact that he was a seasoned festival-goer from me was still very much up for discussion, but that didn't make the truth sting any less. It was ridiculous: I would rather spend a week living the authentic life of an Aberdeen Angus than attend another rock festival, yet there was no getting away from it: *I* wanted to be the one who showed Petter his first festival experience. *I* wanted to have seen him headbang for the first time. *I* wanted to meet Raf. Jealousy overwhelmed me and, in the car on the way back to Crouch End, I did something that no self-respecting adult should do in the presence of a fourteen-and-three-quarter-year-old boy: I sulked.

Sulking, of course, was a wholly pointless activity in the vicinity of Petter. Over the few months that I'd got to know him, I'd found that he was proficiently out of tune with my emotions. He'd never once asked me if I was alright, what I'd been up to the day before, how the sale of my house was progressing, or whether I'd recovered from my bout of laryngitis. I hadn't actually *had* a bout of laryngitis since I'd known him, but that wasn't the point: I still felt upset that he hadn't asked me about it. And now, as I silently negotiated Greater Reading's industrial sprawl, muttering only the most cursory 'oh's and 'mnngh's in response to his eulogies about Rammstein's new video and Raf's new footwear, I found that my brooding was having the exact opposite effect to its intended one. He was becoming *more*, not less, garrulous. He was talking to me as if I was one of his mates.

He was talking to me as if I was one of his mates.
He was talking to me as if I was one of his mates.
I *was* one of his mates.

Clinically and beautifully, the truth stood up and made itself known. Metaphorically, I shook myself down and threw my funk out of the car window (my internal one, that is; my Sly And The Family Stone tape wasn't going anywhere). What did I think I was achieving by getting in a huff with someone half my age? What, precisely, was I mad about? Six months ago, I would have walked recklessly out in front of a double-decker bus just to avoid someone who looked like Petter. Now we laughed and joked together, shared bags of pickled onion Monster Munch, and knew the names of one another's best friends. I should have been rejoicing, not fuming. Here I was, lucky enough to witness a teenager – a slightly melancholy and spoilt teenager, but when all was said and done a good-hearted, mild, funny teenager – in the prime of adolescence, halfway between wanting to be like everyone else and wanting to be unlike everyone else. Sometimes I felt like I wasn't really close to him; sometimes I felt like my musical lessons went in one ear and out the other. But what right *had* I to be close to him? Who, in the end, got properly close to any teenager? Who, in the end, got any teenager to give them an honest acknowledgement that they were interested in Boring Adult Things? You only had to flick through the writings of Elizabeth Fenwick and Dr Tony Smith to realise that it was hard work. My initial Thunderbolt And Lightfoot fantasy might have transformed itself into a Thundergoth And Gordon Lightfoot reality, but I was doing okay. I'd kept him occupied, and that was a big part of Jenny's point in the first place, wasn't it? And now here was Petter, in his element ('element' in this case meaning cleanest AC/DC t-shirt and black nail varnish), and here was me wanting to see him more in his element, and that had to be a good sign, didn't it? I'd forced him into lifts with ageing rockers. I'd cajoled him up trees with folk-loving space cadets. I'd introduced him to a man in tights. Perhaps most fearsomely of all, I'd driven him around the outskirts of Hull. But he was still here, talking to me like I was more than some prematurely middle-of-the-road friend of his family who didn't figure in his day-to-day existence, and that fact alone was enough to make me want to reach out and pat him on the shoulder . . . or certainly enough to reach across charitably and turn Slipknot's 'Eyeless' up a notch on the car stereo. So that's exactly what I did. And for just a few small moments, before I realised that, even mid-revelation, a hideous racket is still a hideous racket, and, seeing him looking the other way, sneakily turned it back down again, guess what?

It very nearly felt tolerable.

EDUCATING PETER

MY GENERATION

'How does that song go? That one you had on in the car before. "People try to put us down, just because we stay around"? I like that.'

'Mmm. It's not one of the best Who songs, but it's okay, until you've heard it for the three hundredth time. It's actually "get around", but I can see why you might have thought it was "stay". The guy who wrote it's pretty old now. I interviewed him a few years ago. He can't hear very well, and I had an ear infection at the time. The interview was basically just us going "WHAT?", "SPEAK UP!" at each other across the table in this studio that he owns.'

'Is his name Roger Daltrey?'

'No. Daltrey's the singer. Pete Townshend writes the songs.'

'And that other one died this year, didn't he? And he'd been doing cocaine.'

'Yeah. John Entwistle.'

'Weird.'

'Do you think your generation's got a defining song like that?'

'I guess something by Eminem.'

'I thought you didn't like hip-hop.'

'No, er, I kind of do now.'

'Ah, that explains it. I wondered why you kept saying "word" all the time the other day.'

'Mmm.'

'What else, though? You know, songs . . .'

'I guess there's "How You Remind Me" by Nickelback. That's pretty cool, and a lot of people at my school liked it – y'know, even really tragic people who like Christina Aguilera.'

'It doesn't really have much of a message, though.'

'Do we have to have a message?'

'No. I guess not. We had "Here we are now, entertain us", but, when you think about it, that doesn't mean anything, does it?

'But I was wondering how you felt – you know, whether you felt you've been swindled when it comes to the pop culture you get exposed to. And, you know, whether you feel any responsibility about saving the world and stuff.'

'I don't know. Raf's brother – Jonti – he's, like, twenty-four, and he reckons that his generation really fucked up and it's up to us to put it all right. But I'm like, "Why should it be up to us?" I feel like the main thing about my generation is that nobody really feels the same about it. But I suppose, in a way, it's quite cool for us, 'cos, well, people who were a bit older than us didn't have the Internet and stuff.'

'But don't you just use it to access porn? That's

what the teen flicks, like *American Pie*, seem to reckon.'

'Yeah, that's what I said. It's cool.'

'Ha.'

'But no, those films like *American Pie* and *Loser* and stuff, I don't really feel like the kids in those. They're really old now, those films – like three years, some of them – and the kids in them weren't really teenagers anyway. They have loads more fun than us. But they're just really dumb, anyway. I dunno.'

'You seem to have a lot of fun, though. I mean, you have a far more active social life than I did at your age. You do fencing and judo . . .'

'Karate!'

'Yeah, sorry. Fencing and karate and stuff. And you're always at parties doing mad things. I'm surprised there's room for feeling depressed. I mean, it seemed that when I was fourteen it was the weird, unpopular kids who wore black and listened to dark, heavy music. But now it seems like it's the popular kids, too. Or perhaps that's just in your social circle.'

'It kind of is, and it kind of isn't. Er . . .'

'Or maybe it's just that you have two different personalities and you keep them carefully compartmentalised. I mean, you know, you don't wear your black nail varnish for karate, do you?'

'No. Er . . . mmmph.'

'That reminds me. How did that nail varnish remover that my wife gave you work out? Did you get it all off in time for the lesson?'

'Er . . . I guess. Yeah.'

'It's funny: I remember you telling me earlier in the

year that modern goths didn't wear black nail varnish.'

'Really? I don't think so. No. No way.'

'You did. Definitely.'

'No. No way. Black nail varnish is totally cool. Everyone knows that.'

'Oh, okay then. But . . . getting back to what we were saying. Do you ever think about the differences between your generation and my generation?'

'I suppose. Sometimes. I think it would have been kind of cool to have seen Nirvana before Kurt Cobain shot himself. And I like some of the clothes that you see them wearing – y'know, Alice In Chains, and people like that. But I guess it would have been kind of shitty, too. I mean, y'know, Tony Blair's shit, but my mum says John Major and Maggie Thatcher were shitter.'

'And the mobile phones were crap. No text messaging.'

'Yeah. Bummer!'

'But things haven't changed that much, really.'

'I dunno. I think I remember a lot of stuff about the Nineties that my mates don't. Like Caroline – she can't even remember Zig and Zag. I thought everyone remembered Zig and Zag.'

'She is bayse, though, like you say.'

'Yeah. Sooo bayse. Ha! I think I kind of like the past, but I wouldn't want to be in it.'

'I feel the same about hippies. I love loads of hippie music and films and clothes and like to imagine myself in 1971, but in reality it probably wouldn't have been so great. I sometimes call my generation Generation Twat, and there are a lot of idiots in it, but

I think the self-righteous attitudes of hippies are responsible for a lot of the bad stuff. So, I guess, in a way, it's up to *us* to clear up the mess.'

'Mmm. The one thing I hate about being around now is being told by everyone that I should be famous. There are all these things like *Pop Idol* and *Fame Academy* and *Model Behaviour* on telly and you get all these lameos at school saying they're going to be on them. I mean, like, that is sooo lame. Even if you do get on them, nobody's going to give a fuck about you in five years' time. Shut up and get a life.'

'But I thought you *wanted* to be a famous rock star. You still do, right?'

'Er, yeah; a *rock* star. Not a pop star. And anyway, I don't want to be famous; I just want to be cool.'

'And do you feel any cooler after hanging around with me?'

'Er . . . Um . . . Can I get back to you on that?'

EDUCATING PETER

AXE DEMONS

With Petter's new school term starting in earnest, our summer together was coming to an end and our final few adventures took on a frenetic quality that I hadn't quite planned for. This was partly my own fault for taking on a temporary job as manager of Circulus, and partly the fault of Marc Bolan from T-Rex for getting killed too close to the date of Axe Demons, Petter's beginning-of-term concert.

On 16 September 2002, it was exactly twenty-five years since Bolan's girlfriend, Gloria Jones, had driven her Mini into a tree on Barnes Common in West London, killing Bolan and badly injuring herself. I wanted to take Petter to the tree for the anniversary celebrations to witness an unsurpassable, authentic example of rock and roll hero worship. Personally, I found T-Rex repetitive and tediously kitsch, but, taking a democratic standpoint, I hoped that some of Bolan's much-discussed 'stardust aura' might rub off on Petter in the build-up to Goat Punishment's performance at Axe Demons the following Monday.

A couple of weeks before we visited Barnes, I'd realised one of my own musical dreams: to become a rock and roll manager. Over the last half decade, I'd become increasingly frustrated and mystified by Circulus's inability to get a record deal, and even more frustrated and mystified by their inability to get off Circulus Meantime and act concerned about it. Finally, while listening to their latest brilliant demo, something inside me had snapped, and I'd decided that if they couldn't do anything about their scandalous lack of corporate backing, then maybe I could. And even if I couldn't, maybe I could teach Petter something constructive in the process.

'We're not going to be able to pay you, you know,' explained Michael. But this was about love, not money. Besides, I'd read about the great rock svengalis – Peter Grant, Don Arden, Sharon Osbourne – and the job seemed easy enough. Get a mahogany desk roughly the size of Birmingham, dangle a few promoters out of the windows by their legs, pay several hundred teenagers to go and buy your band's debut album, and before you knew it you'd be ordering your jumbo cigars from Harrods. Loveable hippie daydreamers that they were, the root of Circulus's unfulfilled promise seemed obvious to me: they'd never forced themselves on anyone. But now they would have me to do that for them. Petter, meanwhile, would act as The Sundance Kid to my managerial Butch Cassidy.

Our first job was to drum up interest in the band's next gig: a mid-morning, open-air performance at the European Car-Free Day demonstration in London's

Russell Square, with comedian-turned-traveller Michael Palin as compère. Immediately, Petter and I sent out a massive email circular to everyone I knew in the music industry, headed 'BEST UNSIGNED BAND IN THE WORLD!', with details about the gig, a potted biography of the band, and the cunning insertion of the industry buzz phrase 'acid folk'. Then, three minutes later, we sent out another, this time remembering to include the date of the gig.

One of the few good things to be said about having email access to the music industry is that, over time, you pick up some pretty tasty virtual addresses from the ether, and can pretend that you're mates with famous people. Somewhere during my seven years' writing about music for a living, I'd acquired the email address for Peter Jenner, legendary early Pink Floyd manager and psychedelic scenester. Petter and I were thrilled to find that, within moments of my Circulus missive going out, Jenner had responded. We were slightly less thrilled, however, to read the email itself, which featured the lone sentence, 'Please remove me from your mailing list.' Still, an assortment of music editors, A&R men and gig promoters had come back to us, making vague promises to 'swing by and watch a few tunes'. I assumed this meant that they were intrigued.

We began to make notes about strategy – not because we needed to, but because it seemed like a manager-type thing to do. One of the toughest things about planning a strategy for your favourite band is that they *are* your favourite band: you don't really want to change anything about them. Instead, I tried to find ways of playing to Circulus's strengths. Noting that they had rarely performed outside London, Petter and I went to work on getting them an out-of-the-way gig – something that would compliment the pastoral, hippies-in-space-but-sort-of-on-a-farm-at-the-same-time ambience of their latest demo.

'What about getting them to play at my school?' asked Petter.

'But that's not really out of the way, is it? And I thought you ditched your folk night,' I said.

'It's a good ten miles from the centre of London, though.'

'Mmm. No. We need to work on the provinces.'

'What about getting them to play in Snowdonia? How cool would that be? Goat Punishment could support. We could have goats there and everything.'

'Now you're just being silly.'

After ten minutes of cold calling, during which we were turned down by my local village fête, we secured Circulus a last-minute headline slot at a cider shed in Banham, a large-ish village in the South Norfolk wilderness. In the end, Petter and I were surprised at how easy this was to arrange: apparently all we had needed to do was give our management company an intriguing name (Goat Enterprises), emphasise the fact that the band had once been reviewed by the *Guardian*, and pretend that we knew who Headspace – the hot folk band on the Banham scene, apparently – were. I felt sure, though, that our success was largely down to the extremely professional nature of our administrative tactics. These consisted of Petter making the call to the promoter on my behalf, asking to speak to the person in charge, then putting the head of his 'management company' (i.e. me) on the line to do the real, hardcore business negotiations. It was all very intimidating, we felt, and only slightly marred by Petter's habit of loudly crunching Kettle Chips in the background while I sealed the deal.

'Brilliant! A cider shed! Perfect!' responded Michael later that day when I informed him about the gig.

'A cider shed? What would we want to play there for?' asked Emma, later still.

One problem I found with managing Circulus was that it was easy to fall into the trap of thinking of them purely as a collective entity. This was no doubt because they *were* so pure, each member's dress sense, musical taste and sleepy way of looking at the world fitting snugly into a bubble of idiosyncratic 1971 perfection that seemed to insulate them from a harsher reality containing nasty things like bandannas and Pete Waterman. I hadn't bargained for the fact that such gentle, perfect musical creatures might be capable of disagreeing or not communicating successfully with one another.

Nevertheless, I pressed on, despite Emma's reservations.

'Don't worry. I hear it's a really fun place. Apparently there's a zoo and a car boot sale just across the road from the venue.'

'And, like, hopefully we can get hold of some of those laser specs Michael was going to get you all to wear!' added Petter.

'What laser specs?' said Emma.

Exposing Petter to the harsh realities of rock management was something I'd never intended as part of our curriculum, but I could see that he was learning some valuable lessons. He was learning, as I was, that bands didn't always communicate well with one another – even cuddly bands who periodically live together and act like one big chemically enhanced family. He was also learning that it was best not to get your band to say, 'Welcome To European People-Free Day!' to the thirteen people who had made the effort to come out and see you, when those people's attention was in severe danger of wandering towards a man on enormous stilts performing on an adjacent stage. But, most pertinently of all, he was learning that it was a good idea to sort out money matters *before* your band played their gig, not afterwards. I hoped that Petter was learning from my mistakes, yet I also hoped that, were he to abandon his dreams of headlining the London Astoria with Goat Punishment in favour of a more behind-the-scenes role in the music industry, he'd be able to employ my fast-talking Colonel Tom-style as a blueprint for future success.

During Goat Enterprises' three-gig, two-week tenure as the commercial force behind Circulus, the band made a grand total of £67.38, not including travel expenses or replacement mandolin strings. During this time, they'd been ignored by an ageing border collie, Michael Palin and the Reviews Editor of *Mojo* magazine, continued to fail to get a record deal, and endured the misfortune of breaking down on the outskirts of Thetford. Even at my most optimistic and paternal, I had to admit it was all a huge disappointment. Sure, the music biz was experiencing a slump, but you only had to look at the career of The

Stereophonics to realise that anybody could get themselves signed these days. Yet my band were photogenic, skinny, sexy and musically erudite . . . and nobody cared.

Only Petter, it seemed, was coming round to their brand of psychedelic folk. He'd also seemed particularly impressed that the band had been paid entirely in cider for their final gig, and slightly disappointed that he'd had to travel back from Banham to West Norfolk with me in the Ford Focus, rather than to London with Michael, Emma, Leo and the cider in Alice The Retro Ford Escort, who'd now had her midriff bedecked with 200 pictures of Seventies Greek warbler Demis Roussos in a kaftan – a sort of hippie answer to go-faster stripes.

On a chilly Sunday afternoon in early autumn, with the zoo and car boot sale not quite doing the business they had at the height of summer, Banham had provided a perfect example of Norfolk sleepiness – the kind of place where people say, 'Drive you steady, Bore,' as a form of farewell. We'd been slightly disturbed, upon arriving at the cider shed, to find a sign outside reading, in descending order, 'Don't Spook The Horse, Circulus, The Bleach Boys', partly because we'd thought Circulus were headlining, but mostly because it wasn't initially clear whether 'Don't Spook The Horse' was a musical collective or a safety instruction to people in the general area. To our relief, it had transpired that Don't Spook The Horse were a Neil Young tribute band who'd played the previous evening (The Bleach Boys were due to play tomorrow) and that Circulus had the stage to themselves. The gig had been a success, with Goat Enterprises' number one export finishing their set to the sound of twenty-three ruddy-complexioned locals whispering, 'Blimey, go you steady now, Bore – they're even better than Headspace!', but it hadn't been enough to dissuade me from feeling that my continuing guidance would do my friends more harm than good. Petter had looked slightly sad, in a nonchalant kind of way, when I'd announced that Goat Enterprises would be folding, and Circulus Robin had been kind enough to ask the pair of us to stay on for a probationary period, but I had seen that I didn't quite have what it takes to make it in the ruthless yet fatherly world of rock management. There was a limit to how many people's dads I could be, and besides, I had an educational obligation to fulfil.

Two days later, Petter and I, accompanied by Michael from Circulus, made our way down a pavement-free street in a leafy pocket of South West London, two of us doing our best to avoid getting the wide bottom part of our trousers caught on the brambles at the side of the road, the other one lagging a few yards behind, not seeming to care what the wide part at the bottom of his trousers, or the even wider parts in the middle and at the top, got snagged upon. It was to be our last adventure together. After this, Petter would be free, and only time would tell if I'd taught him something useful about rock and roll, or if I'd bumbled along uselessly, wasting his and Jenny's time. Whatever the case, it was impossible to deny the relaxed feeling of end-of-term exhilaration as we rounded the corner where Gloria Jones's Mini had skidded out of control.

If you'd been in one of the cars that nearly knocked us into the undergrowth that day you might have been busy thinking about the stock market, or whether your spouse would have sex with you that night, or what wankers pedestrians were, but just maybe you might have wondered what these three people were doing: the man in the wide-brim hat and Cuban heels who looked like a Seventies singer-songwriter but slightly like a movie villain as well, the man in Seventies golf clothes, and the kid accompanying them in the big jacket and bigger trousers. I liked to think we made for a perplexing sight, but in the end we probably looked like three people going to pay their respects at the site of Marc Bolan's death.

I'd expected Bolan's tree to be full of frizzy-haired men with glitter stuck to their faces, wearing platform heels. In reality, what we mostly spotted were tracksuits: blue ones, purple ones, red and yellow ones, even shiny ones, but tracksuits all the same. It was quite possible that we'd missed the big celebrations earlier in the day and caught the less fanatical tourists who slunk along afterwards, but that didn't make it any less depressing. We'd arrived here with irreverence on our minds, but now we looked like the biggest T-Rex obsessives in town. Both Michael and I usually wore Seventies clothes from second-hand stores, but we'd imagined that they were the kind of Seventies clothes that signified a *specific kind* of Seventies music fan. In this setting, however, they just made us look like Seventies People – or, even worse, Bolan People.

'Oh. Are you going to the tree?' a teenage girl clutching a Penguin Classic had asked us as we'd crossed the bridge approaching the famous site. 'Cooool. I've just been there. There's a totally, like, mystic vibe. I wanted to stay longer and light some candles, but I've got yoga class tonight.'

'Well, we'll er . . . light one for you,' I replied, before wincing in the direction of Michael.

'Did she know you?' asked Petter, a moment later.

'No,' I said. 'Never seen her before in my life. Why do you ask?'

'No reason,' he mumbled.

The tree itself didn't look all that threatening: you certainly couldn't imagine it going around murdering glam rockers. Beneath it was a guest book, a bust of Bolan, which in reality looked more like the bust of Val Kilmer's Native American spirit guide, and a selection of flowers and poetry. Crouching down next to a Polish girl in a shell suit with abnormally sharp elbows, Petter and I examined some of the eulogies to the dead singer, almost all of which seemed to feature the word 'star' and a selection of clumsily scattered T-Rex song titles. Our five favourites were, in ascending order:

> Marc, you were a joy
> To behold
> You brought us a TELEGRAM
> And that's wicked cos my middle name is SAM
> But you never really want away did you
> And I imagine your still giving your
> HOT LOVE

In heaven
Are there Rolls Royce's they're?
All my love,
Jackie – Tunbridge Wells

Somewhere, in the night sky, a star shines so bright. Is it you, or is it kryptonite? I seeked you ought, and hoped that you found me, but you didn't, but then again however though in a way I always thought you did. Your own little star (that setlist you gave me is in a framed now).
My never dead devotion,
Wesley 'Faster Than Most' Saeka – Madrid (46)

Metal Guru, is it true?
Riding a white swan, is it fun?
Telegram Sam, are you a man?
Getting it on, is it done?
I know it is. Because it's you. Marc, it's you.
See you in another twenty-five years,
The Dandy In The Underworld, Stockport

Rock gods came down. They gave us a star. A little one only, but she shined bright. Thank you for making those young years such a treasure to behold. Love and glitter – Marquette, 47, Essex

Marc, you had silly hair and you were sort of pudgy – especially in the later photos
Your songs all had the same tune
And you weren't a patch on David Bowie
The band Cornershop once told me Dandy In The

Underworld was a lost classic
But I bought it for £1.50 and it was just as dull as all
your other albums
That said, I did once dance to Get It On when I was
really pissed
All my indifference,
Tom (27), Norfolk

Petter seemed to know more about Bolan than many of the other old-time stars who had featured in our studies. He'd seen him perform on *Top Of The Pops 2* and was slightly curious about his hair ('How does he get it to look so cool when it's, like, so frizzy?'), but was as unmoved by T-Rex's music as I was. Michael, meanwhile, liked Bolan's early hippie strumming but hated the later glam stuff. Still, the three of us tried to keep a tight volume on our blasphemy. It was clear that there were people here who genuinely cared about Bolan – people who, despite their tracksuits, felt like they were a part of him. We didn't exactly want to get into a conversation with them or be their telegram buddies, but we didn't want to get kicked in the throat by them either.

As we made our way back across the common, I reflected on how well Petter now seemed to be getting on with my friends – particularly Michael. Ostensibly, the two of them had very little in common: Michael was a cheery folk musician who liked to buy waistcoats and go on walks in the West Country; Petter was a heavy metal fan who liked to buy t-shirts with pretend blood on them and go on walks around Camden Market. Yet, ever since they'd tied carrots to balloons and shot them together, something subtle yet adhesive within their personalities had gelled.

These days, I thought of Michael as a paragon of human goodness, musical taste and quality clothing. But I wondered if, at fourteen, or even seventeen, I would have got on as well with him as Petter was doing now. Vague memories came back of writing people's entire personalities off, purely on the basis that they hadn't ever attended Rock City's Punk Night. My indie élitism had known few boundaries in the early Nineties, and I'm sure Petter's nu-metal élitism knew equally few now, but the fact that he could find respect for sunny Michael somewhere in his gothic heart at least showed that there was hope for the future. He wasn't going to be trading in his combat pants for a pair of corduroy flares any time soon, but he might, one day. I liked to think of it as another kernel of taste I'd planted in his brain, waiting to blossom in a more mellow time.

By now, Petter had met a dozen or more of my friends, yet I was still to meet one of his. Shortly, however, I'd meet virtually all of them: Raf, Caroline, Zed, Jonti, Sam, Sally, Cauliflower Head and many, many others I'd forgotten but who had no doubt at one point done something really funny involving putting a pair of pants on their head. I thought back to my own school, and the fact that I'd lost touch with everyone I'd known there. At sixteen, when I left school, I'd been impetuous, judgemental, and keen to start a new life and get away from a tiny North Nottinghamshire world where not dropping your 'h's and using big words like, say, 'typical' qualified you for status as a 'posh twat'. But I'd also been to school with some nice people: I know I hadn't meant to lose touch with *everyone*. Did most young adults experience this phenomenon? It seemed so, from talking to my current circle of friends. Wasn't this why friendsreunited, the website that helped put people in touch with old acquaintances from their youth, was so popular: because there were so many people like me out there, entering their late twenties, getting over whatever petty snobbery had governed their social actions, and just wanting to hang out with some nice, wholesome folk they felt comfortable with? How many of Petter's friends would he fade away from over the next few years because of their differing taste in music or politics or clothes or food or drugs or nightclubs or shops? And would he regret it? And should I warn him, or just let him get on with it?

This was Petter's power over me: he turned me into a wistful, dewy-eyed wreck. It wasn't just that I thought about how my musical tastes had changed when I was in his company; I thought about how everything about me had changed. Alarmingly often, before or after, I would find myself emailing a close friend and dropping subtle memories or enquiries about my old self into the text. Stuff like, 'Do you remember Ellie's parties? Is it just me, or do you miss those days at all? Call me stupid, but I *liked* sleeping with a basketball instead of a pillow . . .' and 'Did I really used to wear that Jacob's Mouse t-shirt over a sweater, or is it just my imagination?' I didn't exactly miss my teenage self; I was just abnormally interested in him. Whether it was because I hadn't been to a nightclub in nearly two years, or because, at twenty-seven, I finally felt that I couldn't delay entering fully fledged adulthood any longer, I wasn't sure. There was, however, a definite sense of leaving something behind.

That night – the night before Axe Demons – I made two lists: one featuring things that I liked as a teenager but didn't like now, the other featuring things that I liked now but had scorned as a teenager. Then, when I'd folded them up and put them in an envelope marked 'To Be Opened In September 2012', I made a further two lists: one featuring the passions that I thought Petter might abandon in his twenties, the other featuring those that I thought he might hold on to.

Stuff That I Liked Then But Don't Give A Toss About Now included:

Chicken Ceylon

Special Brew

Carter The Unstoppable
    Sex Machine

Cut-off golf trousers

Punk rock

Stella Artois

Doc Martens

Bedroom wall murals

Tiny, dirty coffee houses

6p indie crisps

America

Girls in black lipstick

Vegans

Stuff That I Like Now But Hated Then featured such unhip pleasures as:

Friends	Bachman-Turner Overdrive
Slippers	Britain
Normal golf trousers	Chicken Rogan Josh
Adult-oriented rock	Girls in normal lipstick
Habitat furnishings	Historical novels
Starbucks	TV cookery
Kettle Chips	

Stuff That Petter Likes Now But Might Tire Of In A Few Years featured:

Slipknot	Saying, 'It was really
Computer games	funny . . .'
Text-messaging	Tattoos
Putting pants on his head	Trouser chains
Smirnoff Ice	

Stuff That Petter Likes Now And Might Still Like In A Few Years included:

Buffy The Vampire Slayer	Cheap Trick
AC/DC	Beer
Crisps	*The Simpsons*
Cadbury's Heroes	*The Osbournes*
Circulus	Goats

I did think, briefly, of making another list – Things That Petter Hates Now But Might Like In A Few Years' Time – but by this stage I was slightly tired of making lists. I'd had a couple of beers, and the whole exercise would probably seem fairly pointless in the morning. I toyed briefly with the idea of giving the last two lists to Petter, but thought better of it, opting instead to keep them for a few years and surprise him with them. I hoped I'd still be in touch with him when he grew up, and I was pretty certain my predictions, whether wrong or right, would prove to be a more interesting barometer of changing tastes than what I'd put in the envelope addressed to my thirty-seven-year-old self. I'm not sure I really believed late-thirties Tom would be very different from his late-twenties equivalent.

But while I was changing less than ever, the trans-formations in Petter's life seemed rapid and alarming. I'd only known him for six months, but in that time he'd grown an inch or two in height and three times that much in hair. He'd also decided hip-hop wasn't crap after all, campaigned at his mum for his first tattoo, bought a coat as long as the one in his self-portrait, and – I suspected – become just a little bit more lenient in his loathing of psychedelic folk music. I found it all quite nauseatingly touching, and never more so than when Goat Punishment took the stage at Axe Demons for their rendition of AC/DC's 'Sin City'.

The first thing I noticed at Axe Demons was just how big and mature Petter looked compared to the other kids of his age. In fact, no, that's wrong. The first thing I noticed at Axe Demons was one of the parents – one half of a famous Eighties electro pop duo. The *second thing* I noticed was just how big and mature Petter looked compared to the other kids of his age. Everywhere you looked, there were half and three-quarter versions of Petter: kids carrying the same thoughtful, melancholy aura, but on a less gangly frame. Some of them wore their hair in spikes and squeaked out nihilistic punk songs that they'd written themselves. Others paced around the stage with bad posture and belted out note-perfect versions of songs by Hole, American Hi-Fi and Offspring. The boys were scruffy, but in a deliberate way. The girls were lean, with good complexions and an affable manner. Just one kid brought a more grown-up element to proceedings: a bigger version of Petter, with longer hair, a longer coat and a longer chain on his trousers, he hid behind the drum kit as a couple of kids an eighth of his size strummed the opening chord sequence to Nirvana's 'Lithium'. Then, without warning, he leapt out over the drum stool, pacing the stage like a caged animal, screaming, 'Yeah, Yeah, Yeah!' at the impressed yet somewhat quizzical-looking artists, college lecturers, archaeologists and TV chefs in the front row. I'd guessed who he was before Jenny had even opened her mouth.

'That's Raf,' she said. 'A few of the parents are a bit scared of him.'

'Yes, I can see why,' I said. 'That metal thing sticking out of his eyebrow could be a liability in a rugby scrum.'

'As you probably know, Petter really looks up to him.'

'Well, yeah. Raf was the one who got him into Nirvana, wasn't he?'

'I worry about the two of them sometimes, but I suppose everyone's got to have a role model.'

'Yeah. I'm sure he's quite harmless underneath all that hair . . . It is hair, isn't it?'

What was most astonishing about Axe Demons wasn't just the level of musical quality on show, but the level of encouragement. No matter how many combinations of musicians took the stage, a hardcore gaggle of teen supporters remained seated on the floor at the front, always applauding, always patting backs, always wishing their friends good luck. These were supposed to be teenagers, for god's sake! They weren't supposed to be this enthusiastic . . . this musical . . . this . . . *happy*.

The moments of self-doubt came one after another. I questioned what I'd been doing, trying to give Petter a musical education when it was quite clear he had a perfectly good one right here. I questioned why Petter had barely said a word to me all night. But then – and I don't say this lightly, since someone was singing an Alanis Morissette song at the time – I relaxed. Petter was back in his natural habitat now, and it was up to me to leave him to it. My job was done, and I'd done okay. Sure, in a few days' time I'd be back at home, listening to Steve Miller or watching *Friends* while wearing a fuzzy dressing gown, or in Norwich, walking on the other side of the street to some slack-jawed insult to innocence in a baseball cap. But the fact was, I'd faced my fear. I'd looked a quintessential example of Teen right in the crisp-stuffed face, asked the big question of myself, and the answer had come through loud and clear: 'I can spend time in the company of this – just.' Not only that, I'd done it at the time in my life when I was most likely to be repelled by my subject – the time when I was furthest away from my own adolescence, yet not quite into thirty- and forty-something living and the inevitable kid-sympathy that comes with it. And where was I now? In a room with 200 teenagers, some of them singing songs that I would once have left the country to avoid. And how did I feel? Impervious, going on tranquil. Petter would remember this night for one reason or another – a girl he'd asked out, a friendship he'd con-solidated, a new song he'd learned – the evening had that sort of feel to it. But I felt that I'd remember it equally well, if not better. Not for the music (though it was surprisingly enjoyable), not for the food, not for the electro-pop star, not even for Petter or the Blue Oyster Cult CD that I'd hidden in his guitar case, but for the other thing that I'd finally jettisoned: some-thing a little bit tightly wound. Something a little bit backward. Something a little bit nervous. Something a little bit paranoid. Something a little bit male.

Something a little bit teenage.

ACKNOWLEDGEMENTS

The author would like to thank the following:

Peter and Jenny for everything, Edie for the moral support, Steve and Sue Golden for the shine, Ed The T for the tights, Harriet Simms and Pat Tynan for the phone numbers, Jim Eldon for the fiddle, the gentle but psychedelic folk people of Blackheath and Plumstead for the gentleness and firearms, Matt Argues for the angst, Jenny Fabian for the patience, and Darian Wondermint for the tickets.

NICE JUMPER
Tom Cox

'DOES FOR GOLF WHAT *FEVER PITCH* DID FOR FOOTBALL . . .
FUNNY, CLEVER AND ALL-TOO-HORRIBLY TRUE'
William Boyd

During the summer of 1988, something strange and disorientating
happened to Tom Cox: he became a teenager. Then, something
even stranger and even more disorientating happened: despite the
best endeavours of his groovy, under-appreciated parents, regular
exposure to music from an early age and a burgeoning fashion
sense, Tom started to play golf. Lots of it.

Finding himself inexorably drawn to a world of male-bonding
rituals and curious trousers, Tom resisted the temptations of
conventional rock and roll revolution, opting instead to cut a
swathe through the golfing establishment, unnerving his fellow
players with his grungey music taste and games of Hide The Dead
Rodent. On the golf course he felt at home and simultaneously
somehow alienated. But Tom also wanted to be the best, taking
five years out of normal adolescent existence to live, breathe,
walk and talk nothing but the sport he loved.

Original, poignant and highly entertaining, *Nice Jumper* is a book
about one teenager's obsessive search for sporting nirvana in the
wrong-coloured socks.

'HILARIOUS . . . LASHINGS OF INSIGHT, SARCASM AND
SLAPSTICK. FORE!'
James Brown, *Jack*

'THE ONLY BOOK I HAVE EVER READ, AND PROBABLY THE
ONLY ONE I EVER WILL READ, ABOUT GOLF. BUT CERTAINLY
NOT THE ONLY BOOK I WILL EVER READ BY TOM COX. *NICE
JUMPER* IS *CATCHER IN THE RYE* MEETS *CADDYSHACK*'
Julie Burchill

'AS FRANK SINATRA WOULD SING, *NICE JUMPER* GOES
"STRAIGHT DOWN THE MIDDLE". HOW CAN A BOOK ABOUT
TEENAGE BOYS, GOLF AND NOTTINGHAM IN THE EIGHTIES
BE THIS GOOD?'
Caitlin Moran, *The Times*

0 552 77076 0

BLACK SWAN

FALLING OUT OF CARS
Jeff Noon

'JEFF NOON IS A PUNK ALDOUS HUXLEY STRINGING TOGETHER IMAGES AND ODDITIES TO ASSEMBLE AN APOLCAYPTIC DREAMWORLD'
Arena

In a world overflowing with images, how can you tell who you really are?

Marlene Moore wasn't even sure why she accepted the job, except that it gave her the chance to just get in her car and drive. To escape, to keep moving, to maybe find a destination for herself. Now she's journeying around England, a land that becomes stranger and more dreamlike, the further she travels. Slowly, day by day, Marlene is falling prey to a sickness – a disease that seems to change the world around her. And the job itself turns out to be far weirder, and more dangerous, than she ever imagined.

A road novel like no other, *Falling Out of Cars* explores a country, and a psyche, falling off the edge of reality.

'FALLING OUT OF CARS IS PART OF NOON'S CONTINUING REVOLT OUT OF GENRE AND INTO CREATIVE RESISTANCE AGAINST ALL TRADITIONAL FORMS OF FICTION'
Guardian

'THIS IS AN IMMACULATE BRITISH ROAD NOVEL; A MELANCHOLIC, ENIGMATIC ODYSSEY THAT TRANSFORMS OUR BLEAK LITTLE ISLAND INTO AN UNCANNY FANTASY WORLD'
SFX

'FRAGMENTED AND LYNCHIAN, THIS IS A MOURNFUL, ACHINGLY LONELY BOOK PACKED WITH RESONANT, FILMIC IMAGERY. ITS REFUSAL TO RESOVLE ITSELF WILL EITHER IRRITATE YOU OR MAKE PRFECT SENSE'
Sleazenation

'THIS IS CLASSIC NOON – STRANGE, COMPELLING AND DISTURBING'
The List

0 552 99970 9

BLACK SWAN

GLOBAL VILLAGE IDIOT
Dispatches from the turn of a century
John O'Farrell

This week the first pet passports came into effect. Around the country dogs have been hopping into photo booths and trying to look as relaxed as possible, which is not easy when you know you're not allowed on the chair.

Gathered here are the best of John O'Farrell's newspaper columns for the *Guardian* and *Independent*, which saw him win Best Columnist of the Year at the British Liars' Awards. In a hundred highly readable and very funny pieces he tackles every topical issue from mobile phones to the dangers of asteroids: *'Okay, so one huge meteorite wiped out all the dinosaurs, but you have to admit it was incredibly back luck that they were all standing in that exact same spot at the time.'* He also claims that scientists only developed a genetically superior monkey so that it could advertise lapsang souchong instead of PG Tips; that with one punch John Prescott placed himself near the top of the list of the world's hardest ever politicians (way ahead of Shirley Williams and Mahatma Gandhi); and that with the election of George W. Bush, the global village has finally got its own global village idiot.

'HIS WRITING IS ENTERTAINING AND IRREVERENT . . .
REFRESHINGLY SELF-DEPRECATING'
The List

0 552 99964 4

BLACK SWAN

HERDING CATS
John McCabe

In a small town in the south west of England, a brutal turf war is
raging quietly. Rivals of a large pork pie manufacturer are being
dealt with one by one. Caught up in the thick of things is Gary
Shrubble, award-dodging journalist of the town's only newspaper.
Gary has a hunch that this is the Big One, the story that will free
him for ever from the mind-numbing tedium of local reporting.

Enter Tim Power, hot-shot advertiser, whose girlfriend has placed
him on a strict twelve-month relationship test. Dragged
reluctantly into the war, Tim discovers that bad advertising can be
every bit as effective as good advertising, provided you don't
mind upsetting borderline psychopaths along the way.

After being savaged by a very small dog during a burglary,
Alistaire Smythe, the town's sole surviving skinhead, is that very
psychopath. Recently recruited by a man with a vested interest in
the Pork Wars, advertisers, journalists and rival meat producers
are all suddenly ripe for the kicking . . .

'ONE OF THE TEN MEN MAKING THE NOVEL WORTH
READING AGAIN'
Arena

0 552 77090 6

BLACK SWAN

A SELECTED LIST OF FINE WRITING
AVAILABLE FROM BLACK SWAN

99914 8	GALLOWAY STREET	John Boyle	£6.99
99704 8	A SHORT HISTORY OF NEARLY EVERYTHING	Bill Bryson	£8.99
77160 0	PECKED TO DEATH BY DUCKS	Tim Cahill	£7.99
99979 2	GATES OF EDEN	Ethan Coen	£7.99
77076 0	NICE JUMPER	Tom Cox	£6.99
99995 4	HIGH SOCIETY	Ben Elton	£6.99
99679 3	SAP RISING	A. A. Gill	£6.99
99656 4	THE TEN O'CLOCK HORSES	Laurie Graham	£5.99
99847 8	WHAT WE DID ON OUR HOLIDAY	John Harding	£6.99
77082 5	THE WISDOM OF CROCODILES	Paul Hoffman	£7.99
77109 0	THE FOURTH HAND	John Irving	£6.99
99958 X	ALMOST LIKE A WHALE	Steve Jones	£9.99
14595 5	BETWEEN EXTREMES	Brian Keenan and John McCarthy	£7.99
77133 3	MY WAR GONE BY, I MISS IT SO	Anthony Lloyd	£7.99
77103 1	BLESSED ARE THE CHEESEMAKERS	Sarah-Kate Lynch	£6.99
14240 9	THE NIGHT LISTENER	Armistead Maupin	£6.99
77090 6	HERDING CATS	John McCabe	£6.99
99970 9	FALLING OUT OF CARS	Jeff Noon	£6.99
99964 4	GLOBAL VILLAGE IDIOT	John O'Farrell	£6.99
77095 7	LONDON IRISH	Zane Radcliffe	£6.99
99645 9	THE WRONG BOY	Willy Russell	£6.99
99122 8	THE HOUSE OF GOD	Samuel Shem	£7.99
99952 0	LIFE ISN'T ALL HA HA HEE HEE	Meera Syal	£6.99
99638 6	BETTER THAN SEX	Hunter S. Thompson	£6.99
99997 0	DUENDE	Jason Webster	£7.99
99891 5	IN THE SHADOW OF A SAINT	Ken Wiwa	£7.99